Advance Praise for Hiring Right

"Simon Parkin is regarded by many including his peers to be a leading expert and thought leader in the talent and recruitment space. Simon challenges the status quo, often being disruptive and thought provoking. Simon has helped to influence the recruitment movement towards customer centric thinking and leveraging data & analytics to draw out deeper insights. Simon has mentored and shaped the careers of many global recruitment leaders including myself. Simon is the guru global recruitment leaders go to for advice." • **SHANE CREAMER, GLOBAL TALENT ACQUISITION LEADER, GLOBAL FINANCIAL SERVICES ORGANIZATION**

"Simon's expertise is second to none. This comes from his own experiences both as a leader in recruitment and as a leader in the industry. He has been able to get to know countless organizations and leaders, and from these connections fortifies his knowledge now available to us all in this great book. It is a gift for anyone who makes hires regardless of the role they play. Hiring Right lays out recruitment and hiring in a way that grasps the traditional "musts" yet also reaches new territory and key trends as we all evolve in the talent acquisition space. Big thanks to Simon" • **COREY BROOKS, GLOBAL TALENT ACQUISITION BRANDING LEADER, GLOBAL TECHNOLOGY ORGANIZATION**

"Simon brings together his deep recruitment and hiring experience in Hiring Right to address the changing market trends in support of your most important asset for your business success – your people!" • **KEVIN HENDERSHOT, PRINCIPAL, MERCER CANADA**

"Simon is a true leader in his field. His practical approach to talent management and networking sets him apart from others in his field. He stays connected to new trends and offers innovative approaches to Human Resources challenges. He is an engaging collaborator who shares his expertise with generosity." • **REHANA DOOBAY, VICE PRESIDENT HR, GLOBAL PHARMACEUTICAL ORGANIZATION**

"In Hiring Right, Simon Parkin does a great job using his vast recruiting experience to provide guidance on how to build an effective and current recruiting program. He goes into detail on the importance of customer alignment, having the right tools, and building an empathetic and authentic approach to candidate interactions." • **JESPER BENDTSEN, GLOBAL TALENT ACQUISITION LEADER**

"What makes Simon special is the investment he makes to truly understand your overall business strategy and needs and his commitment to work with your business to craft a talent acquisition strategy that is unique to your organization. Working with Simon, I found that he uses his overall HR expertise and business acumen to effectively contribute to our corporate talent management strategy. His dedication and enthusiasm to recruitment and hiring are exemplary and his dedication to keeping abreast of emerging talent acquisition trends and best practices is remarkable." • **DETA CONSTANTINE, CHRO, GLOBAL TECHNOLOGY ORGANIZATION**

HIRING RIGHT

HIRING RIGHT

*How to Turn Recruiting Into
Your Competitive Advantage*

Simon Parkin

Founder, The Talent Company, a Career Partners International firm

BRIGHTFLAME BOOKS, TORONTO

TABLE OF CONTENTS

PART 3 — EXECUTION
161

By Maura Dyer,
Talent Acquisition Executive

When I began my career many years ago, Recruitment was a tactical function focused on sourcing and selecting candidates to fill seats. Recruiters were order takers, and recruitment leaders were focused solely on the number of hires their teams made. There were however a few recruitment and business leaders who saw the strategic importance of hiring right.

These leaders understood how a bad hire could negatively affect the bottom line, their employment brand, and ultimately, their consumer brand. So, they created competitive advantage by building great recruitment teams that find, engage, and secure the best talent for their market.

I first met Simon when he interviewed me for a role on his team. It was clear that he was one of these forward-thinking recruitment leaders. We talked passionately for hours about what makes a great recruiter, how the power was shifting to candidates, how to better support hiring managers in making the right decisions, their expectations (realistic and unrealistic!), how technology impacted the recruitment process, and most importantly, how to positively engage candidates during the recruitment process. It was refreshing to hear about how Simon saw the candidate as a stakeholder who should be at the centre of the recruitment process – similar to how customers are viewed in the most successful consumer businesses. He understood that recruiters must be both marketing and sales professionals focused on quality of hire. I was hooked on his vision.

Over time, recruiting has continued to become much more complex. But the problem isn't just that top talent is in demand. Demand now exceeds supply; recruitment technology isn't just a tool for efficiency, it has advanced to the point that much of the hiring process can be automated; and candidates are not just central to the process, they are now in control. It's no wonder we still haven't gotten it right and it's only going to get harder. With most companies stating talent as a top priority, we must shift our thinking from filling vacancies efficiently to being proactive in identifying great talent. It is also time to stop neglecting and disengaging our candidates and to start facilitating a great experience.

Easier said than done. Or is it?

In *Hiring Right*, Simon shares his straightforward and proven approach to building an efficient, simple, and cost-effective recruitment process. His focus is set on seeking out and engaging the best candidates while providing them a positive experience – balancing both efficiency and effectiveness. If you're looking for practical and actionable tactics to become a better recruiter, hiring manager or recruitment leader, this book is for you. Simon has always been my go-to thought partner when I faced recruitment challenges, and now he's sharing his best practices and learning with you.

Good luck on your path to hiring right. You're in great hands.

Recruiting Has Changed

"Stand clear!"

I jumped to the side as a young guy in a suit leapt over the turnstile and ran to the exit. The heavy revolving glass door slowed him down, and for a moment I wondered whether I should try to stop him. I realized, however, that the security guard who had shouted the warning was laughing, so I just stood and watched as the "runner" pushed the ridiculously slow door. As soon as there was a gap big enough, he sidled out and—without even a glance back—disappeared into the lunchtime crowds milling past the entrance to the building.

As I introduced myself at the front desk, the receptionist must have seen the bewildered look on my face. "It's assessment day," she shrugged, as though that would somehow make things clearer.

It didn't.

It's not the kind of question you expect to ask your boss on the first day in a new job, but I had to know. So, once I'd been shown into his office and we'd exchanged the usual pleasantries, I told him what had happened, and about the receptionist's cryptic comment.

He chuckled. "You get used to that around here," he said, with a twinkle, "especially in this job."

Candidates had to take an hour-long computer-based assessment—I knew that, because I'd been through the process myself. They would come to the office and sit in front of a computer to take the test. At the end, one of two things would happen. Either a message would flash up to say they'd passed and would be proceeding to the next stage of the process, or a different message would appear informing them that they had failed and would be escorted from the building.

That was when some of them would decide they didn't want to be thrown out onto the street like a bum, so they would walk, run, or even—as I'd seen today—leap out of the building.

On the way out, those candidates would pass posters and brochures inviting them to become customers. But why would any of those people ever want to buy from the company after that experience? What's more, they would go home and tell their friends and family about how badly they'd been treated and those people, in turn, would be unlikely to become customers.

And what if the candidate wasn't suitable for that position, but could have been a good candidate for a future role? Again, they would be unlikely to consider it. And if a friend ever said "I'm thinking of working for that company," what advice do you think the candidate would give them?

The company had lost not just a job applicant but future buyers and candidates also, and it had put a very negative message out into the market about what it was like to deal with them.

Much of this book focuses on the experience we create for applicants, candidates, and eventually new hires. How we design the recruitment process is a key determinant of which candidates we can attract, make offers to, and ultimately bring into the organization.

The Balance of Power Has Shifted

Over the course of my career, I have seen many changes in the world of recruitment. In recent years, however, those changes have become seismic.

The biggest development—and one which is at the heart of this book—is the power shift that has taken place.

When I began my career, employers held all the cards. People tended to stay in jobs for a long time, which restricted the "supply" of opportunities. It was the candidate who first had to convince a company to interview them and then had to convince the interviewer to hire them. It was hard for candidates to find out about the best roles, hard for them to find out about the company they hoped to work for, and hard for them to compare what they were offered to what others in the market were getting.

Because of developments that I'll discuss in this book, however, that world is gone. Today's candidates are better prepared than any that have come before, and the best of them are in high demand. They come to interview knowing more about the company than many interviewers, with detailed knowledge of what they should be offered (and often with their own ideas and expectations of what it will take to entice them to accept a job), and with a seemingly uncanny understanding of what it's like to work for the company—both the good and the bad.

If you are involved in recruiting in any way, you need to adapt to this new world. You cannot afford to ignore the changes, and you cannot simply go on doing what you have always done.

With growing competition for the best candidates, attracting, closing, and retaining talent has become a critical success factor for organizations, and it can make the difference between a company that survives and thrives, and one that does not.

And yet, as you'll see in *Hiring Right*, hiring managers do not get the training and support they require, recruiters continue to act as though nothing has changed, and both insist on treating candidates as though they are fortunate the company is even considering them.

Recruitment Needs Champions

While I was researching this book, I gave a keynote speech for an audience of 150 HR managers where I set out the broad principles of what you are about to read.

About a third of them followed up with me over the following days to thank me. They are so used to people talking about talent acquisition in a very complicated way, that they were happy someone was finally giving them a workable approach.

On the one hand, I was delighted that the ideas were so well received. On the other, I was shocked that they didn't know all of this already. After all, recruiting isn't rocket-science!

Back in 2014, The Talent Company published a study called the *HR Pulse*. We surveyed not just HR professionals but also business leaders. Business leaders told us that their top priority from HR is talent acquisition and they need the organization to be better at hiring. When the HR group gave us their priorities, however, talent acquisition wasn't even in the top three. That's an interesting—and troubling—mismatch.

Few organizations make recruiting the strategic priority it needs to be. Companies that spend millions creating a customer-facing brand neglect the message they are presenting in the employment market—their employer brand—and create candidate experiences that jar with the customer experience they have often invested heavily to create.

The result? Disengaged candidates who will literally run from the building to get away and would rather work anywhere else but there, poor hiring decisions that bring the wrong person into the organization, and stressed recruiters juggling unrealistic requests from clueless hiring managers.

Recruitment goes far beyond sourcing and selecting new employees. The impact of bad hires can be toxic to the teams they join, but it also has very real effects on the bottom line of the organization. A poor recruiting process that creates a negative candidate experience can hurt the employer brand, and overt time that can damage the company's consumer brand. Correcting hiring mistakes is usually a difficult, expensive, and lengthy process during which work is not getting done and team and organizational effectiveness suffer.

The Future of Recruitment

Going forward, the critical factor for recruitment will be connecting to individuals. We have access to a vast pool of talent for every position. Technology makes it possible for us to identify, find, and engage the best candidates wherever in the world they may be—in ways that were impossible just a few years ago.

So, organizations need to become more proactive in approaching potential employees. Recruitment is still a very transactional and reactive function. Most organizations wait until a position becomes open before they start to think about how to fill it, rather than planning and taking the time to understand who they will need to attract in the future and creating relationships with those people in advance.

Recruitment also needs to break free of the shackles of the job description. Candidates are hardly ever a 100% match for a these, and hiring managers struggle to compare strong candidates who inevitably have different gaps in their skills and experience and usually have unique strengths and potentials that aren't captured in the job description.

Successful organizations of the future will stop letting the job description dictate who they hire and who they reject, and instead focus on finding great talent and designing jobs to leverage the assets an individual can bring to the role, the team, and the organization as a whole.

The Opportunity for Recruiting

The good news for you is that every organization—including your competitors—is facing the same challenges. That creates a massive opportunity: the first organization in a market or industry to adapt to those challenges and changes will create a commanding competitive advantage over other employers.

Getting your recruitment processes right doesn't just mean you attract the best job seekers for your open positions. It also puts you in a position to seek out the best candidates in the market—even ones who are already employed—engage them in an ongoing conversation, and bring them into your workforce when the opportunity arises. That, in turn, means you'll be able to hire the best people before your competitors have even found out they were open to changing jobs.

In a world where many organizations emptily proclaim that people are their greatest asset, this new way of recruiting will allow you to turn those platitudes into reality.

The Big Idea

Great recruiters think like sales and marketing people: their job is not merely to post a job and wait to see who applies, it is to go out into the market, start conversations, and hunt for the top prospects. And if you want great recruitment in your organization, it starts with having great recruiters.

To prepare your recruiters and hiring managers for this new mindset, this book presents a model for finding, engaging, closing, and retaining the top candidates and high performers in your market.

Hiring Right is broken down into three parts.

In Part One, Trends, I examine how recruitment has changed and what those changes mean for the future. I look at how candidate attitudes and expectations have evolved, how technology has impacted both sides of the job hunt—the employer and the candidate—and how increasing pressure on recruiters and hiring managers alike is making the task of hiring the right person harder.

In Part Two, The Model, I present a new way of thinking about and managing recruitment. I set out an end-to-end process based on over 20 years managing talent acquisition for a number of blue-chip organizations and running the firm I founded, The Talent Company.

In Part Three, Execution, I offer practical instructions and advice for implementing the model in your own organization.

What you learn by reading *Hiring Right* will make it easier to hire great talent. None of this is theory or blue-sky thinking. Throughout the book you'll see examples—some inspirational, others cautionary—drawn from daily life at the companies I have worked with. My hope is that you will find yourself thinking "a-ha!" at various points, nodding in recognition at others, and highlighting, underlining, and scribbling notes in the margin in every chapter.

PART ONE

Trends

CHAPTER 1

Why Hiring Is Getting Harder

Organizations face a growing number of common challenges, and recruiters are under more pressure than ever. Never before has an organization had such broad reach and open access to candidates and the opportunity, in effect, to approach anyone they want.

Not so long ago, if you needed to fill an open position you had two options. Either you put an ad in the newspaper—a model of recruitment I call 'post and pray'—or you hired a head hunter who had company lists, and they would call into organizations the old-fashioned way and ask to speak to "the marketing manager" (or whatever role you were hiring).

If you were lucky, your posting would attract 10-15 applications and the recruiter's job was to talk to those candidates and identify the best among them. Today, a job posting is more likely to attract 100-200 applications, but organizations haven't increased their recruiter headcount to match. And recruiters aren't just dealing with more applicants; they're also having to handle more roles. In our 2016 *Talent Acquisition Practices Study*, The Talent Company interviewed over 300 Recruitment and HR leaders from 155 organizations across the United States and Canada. We found that the average recruiter is now working on 30 to 40 open opportunities at any given time.

Because of those two changes, recruiters don't have time to talk with every candidate face-to-face. Indeed, most of them can do little more than manage the flow of candidates through the company's applicant tracking system.

Organizations haven't adjusted to this new world because of budget constraints and lack of prioritization. A recent study by PwC found that 63%

of CEOs worry that the availability of key skills will undermine their strategies and plans for growth, and 93% of CEOs recognize the need to change their strategy for attracting and retaining talent[1]. That means that recruiters—and the organizations they work for—need to adapt to the changes in their world. Unfortunately, the reality is that the Recruitment function in most organizations is not seen as a strategic priority, so it's often underfunded and starved of resources.

Recruitment has always been low on the totem pole within HR, and historically many organizations have seen it as an entry level HR job for new graduates. That is finally changing, and recruiter salaries are now among the highest in HR. You can't hire a recruiter for $40,000 a year anymore, and recruiters with more than a couple of years' experience typically command salaries of at least double that. Unfortunately, that also means that growing the Recruitment function requires more investment.

Why Is It So Hard to Find Good Candidates?

Companies like Apple, Google, and Microsoft have no problem attracting hundreds of candidates for every open position. Many of the organizations I work with also have a great employer or consumer brand, and people want to work for them. But the *good* people get lost in the volume.

When you have three or four hundred applicants for every role, and your recruiters are working on 30 or 40 requisitions, there's a high probability that your recruiters are having to trawl through résumés as quickly as they can and they can't focus on any individual requisition. If you're lucky, the recruiter understands each role and the most critical criteria for it, but out

---

[1] PwC, 20th CEO Survey, 2017

of 400 applicants they may only have time to look at the first 50. So, if the best applicant happens to be #51, they may not even get seen.

In addition to investing in recruitment talent, organizations also need to invest in systems to support the Recruitment function, like candidate tracking tools, sourcing systems, and licenses for online platforms. Unfortunately, investing in talent acquisition technology isn't enough. Technology alone does not make the Recruitment function more effective, because more tools simply means access to more candidates. Unless you also have more recruiters to manage the increased candidate flow, that just makes the situation worse.

The real challenge is that more candidates doesn't always mean more *good* candidates, so it actually becomes much harder to find which of those hundreds of applicants are the right fit for the opportunity. You can no longer afford to treat recruitment as a numbers game. Organizations used to brag about how many applicants they got for each new job opening. But quantity does not equal quality, and if your Recruitment function is under-staffed and under-financed, they have no hope of identifying the needles in an ever-growing haystack.

When I joined American Express, I'd never been exposed to the high-volume recruiting that is typical in call centers. I came from Accenture, where high-quality applicants are the norm and there were robust hiring processes in place. American Express was the exact opposite. The company would pick from whoever applied, hire them, and train them to an acceptable standard. As a result, the attrition rate was astronomical—50% staff turnover every year—and a lot of money was being spent training people who weren't expected to make it through the first few months. I spent my initial weeks on the job questioning why we didn't just hire people with experience. Over time, I was able to switch the recruiting team's mindset to looking for candidates who matched a profile of the ideal hire and putting them through a rigorous recruitment process.

Within six months, attrition dropped to 15%, customer satisfaction with the call center went up, and the new hires were more comfortable upselling and cross-selling—an essential part of the business model—which fed straight to the bottom line. The training department was happy, and so was the business. It was an easy win, but it set the context for my career at the company: with a significant quantifiable success in such a short period of time, Recruitment was the golden child and it was easier for me to ask for more investment.

Great on Paper

Another major challenge for recruiters is that the best-looking résumés don't always belong to the best candidates, and the best candidates don't necessarily have the best-looking résumés. Many great candidates have terrible résumés, and until a recruiter speaks to them and engages them in dialog, it's hard to know what they are truly like.

How Job Search Has Changed for Candidates

Just as the job search landscape has changed for organizations and recruiters, it has also changed for the candidates. I remember the first job fair I attended at university. I walked into a hall filled with booths: over a hundred organizations were represented, half of which were household name consumer brands and the other half you had never heard of. Students back then didn't leave college with the level of specialization that you see today, and we certainly didn't have a detailed plan of what our life and career would look like. You turned up for the job fair in your best suit, and the mindset was *I need a job. I need to start my career somewhere.* Today, students are already specializing in their first degree or diploma, and they have a far better idea of where they want to work and in what role.

Technology has made it easier for companies to find great candidates. There's a high probability that anyone you might want to hire has an online presence, and tools such as LinkedIn and ZoomInfo allow you to map the talent inside an organization without having to resort to subterfuge.

The flip side of that, however is that those same technological advances have given candidates access to more opportunities and choices than ever before. They have greater insight into organizations and can make better decisions about whether they even want to work for a company before they sit down with an interviewer.

That increased access and information means candidates are better prepared than ever for their interview, with in-depth knowledge of the company and perhaps even the interviewer, and they can use a broad range of apps and tools to prepare in advance. They come with more confidence than ever, and a certain bravado. They know much more about the company than past candidates ever did, and they expect recruiters and hiring managers to be as well-informed about what is happening to the company as they are. In addition, sites like Glassdoor give them insights into the organization that an interviewer may not have, because the candidate is getting the employee perspective about working for the company.

On the whole, today's candidates are also smarter when it comes to preparing for "traditional" interview questions. They know the most common behavioral questions they are likely to be asked, and they have their responses worked out in advance—even if those responses aren't always 100% true. They go into an interview ready to sell themselves and pitch to the interviewer why they should be hired.

At the same time, managers and recruiters need to be prepared for candidates asking very different questions. Twenty years ago, candidates mostly asked about the same basic things: salary, vacation, and benefits. Today's candidates ask far more in-depth questions. They want to know what a day in the role will look like. They want to know what the next career step will be if they get the job. They want to know about onboarding, and training opportunities. Many of them want to know about the community initiatives and charitable work the company organizes. Every candidate has a different perspective on what's important to them, and they aren't afraid to ask.

From an organizational perspective, that creates another headache: it's much harder to weed out the applicants who may not be the best fit for your company when you're looking at a group of people who are better informed than you are and can use that knowledge to sound like they're a better fit than they really are.

The best candidates—and even average ones—need to be wooed; they need to feel that the organization wants them as much as they want the organization. In many ways, it represents the shift from looking for a career for life with the same organization to a more self-aware and self-centered approach that acknowledges the fact that the candidate may not be working for you five years from now, so they need to take care of themselves and their career in a way that past generations of job seekers did not.

Technology Isn't the Solution

As we'll see later in the book, many organizations have turned to technology to manage and automate the recruitment process in the hope that systems would help them deal with the volume. When you talk to candidates, however, it's clear that those systems aren't helping.

One of our clients, an online education platform, engaged us because they were losing too many good candidates as they went through their recruitment process. It was clear that the process was broken, but they couldn't figure out where or how. The problem, it turned out, was simple and it was right at the start: when someone applied for a role there was no acknowledgment. Later, if a recruiter looked at their submission and decided they were suitable, the first contact the candidate would have was a generic system-generated email informing them that the next step was an obligatory two-hour assessment.

Think about that from the candidate's perspective. They saw a job advertised and they have applied for it. They're not even sure their application was received because they didn't get a response. They're not engaged yet, but out of the blue, a few days or a week later, with no prior human contact from the company, they get a cold email telling them they must take a test in order to proceed.

It's not the most engaging candidate experience, and the company was paying the price: other employers, with better ways of engaging the candidate, were stealing their best applicants. Worse still, the company was recruiting from a small community of technical experts, and news was already circulating among that group that it wasn't worth wasting your time applying to them.

That company is, sadly, not unique. In fact, 64% of all job applicants never hear back from an employer after submitting their résumé: we call it "the résumé black hole." The problem is, if every company in a market is doing it (and, let's face it, they are), that encourages candidates to apply to any and every opportunity they see. That means more applicants for every post, and because they don't know whether they'll get a response, candidates aren't being picky: they apply for any job available, whether it's a good fit or not.

The result is a situation where the wrong candidates are applying for your job, and the right candidates are applying for the wrong jobs. Some organizations have responded by abandoning job postings altogether. Instead, they hope their employer brand is strong enough that candidates will submit a résumé on spec. When an application comes in, the recruiter follows up, has an actual conversation, and evaluates where in the organization that person would be a good fit.

Eventually, however, even those companies hit the same road block: the sheer volume those recruiters are faced with makes it physically impossible to talk to every candidate. At that point, their precious employer brand is at risk, because they are promising people they will speak to them, but the recruiters can't keep up.

The Challenge of "Post and Pray"

The traditional recruitment model used by organizations in sourcing potential candidates for open roles is "Post and Pray": recruiters advertise their open roles on job boards and wait for candidates to apply. That gives all the power to the candidates, because they are the ones driving everything that happens: it's the candidate who finds the posting, decides whether they are interested, and takes action to apply.

The problem with Post and Pray is that it is predicated on an unrealistic assumption that because a job is posted publicly everyone will see it. However, research suggests that only about 14% of candidates are actively looking for a job at any moment in time[2], so the recruiter is hoping (and praying) that their ideal candidate is among that 14%, that they will find the listing amongst the other tens of thousands of listings online, and that they will be motivated to apply.

Why, then, do so many recruiters rely on Post and Pray? First, because it's what they've done throughout their career and they don't know how to do anything else. Second, because when they have 30 open positions on their desk, they don't have time to focus on researching and engaging candidates. Often, they'll set up IT systems to automate Post and Pray simply as a way to manage their workload: when a requisition arrives, they click a button, the job gets posted to a board, and they can send an email to the hiring manager to say things are under way.

---

[2] Source: Jobvite 2017

Unfortunately, Post and Pray recruiters don't know how to be more pro-active in their hiring practices. They are used to dealing with candidates who are already interested in the opportunity, and if they have never had to "hunt" before, they don't have the necessary experience, behaviors, or mindset.

Can Post and Pray Deliver the Best Candidates?

None of what I just said means that Post and Pray recruiters can't get the best candidates. After all, every time you buy a lottery ticket, there's a probability—slim as it is—that you could hit the jackpot. The real problem with Post and Pray is that it restricts your ability to develop a large pool of qualified candidates. You are depending on job-seekers to act, and rather than focusing on pursuing qualified candidates, your time is taken up sifting through unqualified ones in the hope of finding someone suitable.

Switching from Post and Pray to a more proactive approach is not a quick fix. It starts with planning. As we'll see in Part Three, it ties into having a workforce plan and identifying the areas of the business that will be growing. And your Recruitment team need to get comfortable with going after candidates.

"Candidates" Not "Applicants"

When I first started my career, recruitment ads went into the newspaper on Tuesday, Thursday, and Saturday and by the next morning you'd have replies from a couple of dozen applicants. You could quickly weed out the ones who shouldn't have applied, and you were left with half a dozen po-tentials. Then it was up to the hiring manager would pick the best applicant out of that group.

The real change in recruitment is that with greater access to candidates, organizations no longer want the best *applicant*. They want the best *candidate* wherever they are in the market. They want to consider 100% of potential hires, not the 14% who might be looking. That shift, however, has to be accompanied by a new mindset in recruiting. It means we have to proactively go out and seek out talent, rather than gambling that they are going to see our posting somewhere *and* be looking at that exact moment.

> The real change in recruitment is that with greater access to candidates, organizations no longer want the best <u>applicant</u>. They want the best <u>candidate</u> in the market.

Building a Sales Mindset

The new market demands a more aggressive approach, one that requires recruiters who know how to create a pipeline of talent that they can hire from, and who know how to influence and sell.

If a candidate isn't looking to change jobs, you can't start talking to them about a role: you first have to sell them the idea of switching. However, most recruiters aren't comfortable picking up the phone and cold-calling candidates to pitch to them. Indeed, it's usually easier to take someone who knows how to sell and teach them how to be a great recruiter than to take a recruiter and teach them sales and marketing.

Salesforce is a prime example of an organization that recognizes that traditional recruiters don't have the competency or capability to hunt. Instead, they are hiring sales and marketing people and teaching them to be recruiters; people who will go out proactively and hunt for candidates rather than posting an ad and seeing who responds.

Their Recruitment function is structured like a sales team, with an inbound acquisition team that responds to inquiries and direct approaches, and an outbound team to reach out proactively to people they've identified in the talent pool.

That's not the only unusual profile you'll find among recruiters. Earlier, I mentioned the value of focusing recruiters on specific sectors. Some innovative organizations are taking that one step further, hiring people with functional expertise and teaching them how to recruit.

Talent Pipelining

Imagine you posted a job and the only applicants were the Three Stooges—Curly, Larry and Moe. Are you going to hire one of them just because that's who is available? Or do you keep the post open and hope that someone better comes along?

Post and pray gives you no control over the quality of applicants, and when you're dependent on applicants to take the initiative, it's easy to end up with a small list of potential candidates. In those circumstances, it can be tempting to assume that your only options are to recruit one of them or to keep the post open and wait for a suitable applicant.

But, if you start instead with a list of a hundred people who meet your requirements in terms of skillset, experience, and companies they've worked for, you can reach out to them knowing that they will be high-quality candidates. So, you're expanding your talent pool with great talent, not just three hundred random under-qualified applicants.

Pipelining—building talent communities and sourcing candidates before you need them—is a theme we explore in detail in Parts Two and Three. As a recruiter when you come across a great candidate—someone who is not only a perfect fit for the organization, but perhaps also has a skillset you need—you should be keeping in contact with them. Even if you don't have an opening for them right at this moment, there might be one a month from now. If that happens, you need to still be on their radar and keeping them engaged.

Creating the Sales Mindset

Business development people are very outcome focused. They operate with the end in mind—which is closing the deal. We need to bring a similar mindset into the world of recruiting. Good recruiters and hiring managers recognize the importance of this way of thinking. Getting the others to change can be harder, though.

Recruiters can't be slaves to the process. For many roles, they may have to go out into the market and find, meet, and assess suitable candidates. The only way to drive that sort of flexibility, and the behaviors to support it, is through incentives. Some organizations, for example, have started tying a proportion of recruiters' and hiring managers' performance pay to the performance of the people they hire. Suddenly, those individuals take a little more care selecting candidates—even the 30-year veterans who would otherwise insist they had nothing to learn when it comes to recruiting.

At American Express, Recruitment costs weren't centralized under HR; each business unit paid for their hires directly, and the better we did, the more investment we got the following year.

When I joined, recruiters were paid a base salary with a traditional corporate bonus tied to the performance of the company as a whole. In the team, I had newer recruiters who had been in place for a year working alongside some very good, highly experienced recruiters.

I was fortunate to have the opportunity to experiment with the compensation models of our Recruitment department. When I offered people the option of taking a lower base with a higher variable incentive based on quality of hire and outcome metrics, the experienced recruiters jumped at the opportunity while the others preferred to stick with the security of their $80,000 base.

We tracked quality of hire across the two groups, and the incented group outperformed the traditionally-compensated ones by a factor of four-to-one. So, when it came to hiring people into high-profile lines of business that had a direct bottom-line impact, I always assigned the work to one of the highly incented recruiters, and it became a virtuous cycle: those profit-driving business groups had an incentive to invest time and energy into recruitment because they were getting more out of it.

Moving Forward

As we've seen, recruiters face increasing pressure from three broad trends that affect their ability to be successful in their role.

First, they are handling more candidates for more roles and they are struggling to keep up with the demands placed on them by the business. PwC's 2017 CEO Survey identified talent as one of the two business priorities for CEOs. However, that isn't translating into more funding for talent: as The Talent Company's own 2016 Talent Acquisition Practices Study found, HR and Talent Acquisition leaders are worried about how they'll be able to meet growing hiring demands without a corresponding increase in overall investment.

Second, employment market dynamics have shifted. Candidates have better visibility of opportunities and possibilities, and they have greater insight into potential employers. That makes it harder for companies to attract the best candidates by traditional methods.

Third, the traditional notion of "an employer for life" and long-term employer-employee loyalty has broken down. As a result, while only 14% of candidates are actively looking for a new job at any given point in time, many more candidates would be open to considering an opportunity if it arose. Those latter candidates cannot be reached by "post and pray" approaches to hiring.

To respond to these trends, three things need to happen.

1) Organizational leaders need to recognize the strategic importance of recruiting and prioritize (and invest in) it accordingly.
2) Recruiters need to adopt a sales/"hunter" mentality. They can no longer afford to post a job listing and wait for suitable applicants to come to them. They have to reach out into the market, find the best candidates, and woo them even before those candidates start thinking about a new position.
3) Companies can't expect to woo a great candidate overnight. The process takes time, so recruiters need to start building pipelines of potential targets in the same way that sales teams build pipelines of prospects.

Reflective Questions

How valued is the recruiter role in your organization? How does that show up day-to-day in the business?

Are your CEO and executive team concerned about the availability of great talent for your organization? Does your organization invest enough in talent acquisition and hiring?

On average, how many candidates apply for your open positions? How many of them would you consider "strong candidates" with the right skills and experience for the roles?

Do you consider your Talent Acquisition function reactive or proactive? Does your Talent Acquisition function rely too heavily on the "Post and Pray"? Does your organization ever pipeline talent for future opportunities?

Does your organization hire the "best applicant" who applies for the role or do they hire the "best candidate" in the market? How aggressive is your Talent Acquisition function in hunting for great talent in the market?

CHAPTER 2

Increasing Focus on "Fit"

Recruitment is no longer just about whether someone can do the job. It's also about whether a candidate is truly the right fit for the team, the organization, the culture, the environment, and even the industry. Most hiring managers are so focused on their immediate need—to fill the current position in their team—that they're not thinking about the candidate's long-term potential within the organization.

Mary, the head of Talent Acquisition at a mid-sized industrial firm, shook her head and looked down at the pile of performance reports she'd been showing me. "I don't get it. James is a great engineer. He went to an excellent school, and he did really well at his last company. But he's just gone to pieces since we hired him. It's been a complete disaster, and company leadership are pointing fingers at the Recruitment team."

I was pretty sure I knew what was happening. I could guess what the company's interview process was like: "Where did you go to school? Tell me about your last job: what did you do?" There would be very few questions about values and beliefs. And if an interviewer asked a candidate "Tell me about a challenge you faced and how you overcame it?" there probably weren't a lot of follow-on questions to probe and dig deeper.

Hiring is about selecting the right person, with the knowledge, skills and ability to perform the job. However, not all hires are successful, and a major reason is that the new employee is not a good *fit*. Anyone you hire into your organization has to be able to function effectively inside the culture. That means that you're not just looking for people whose skills match the job requirements—you're looking for people whose values, beliefs and behaviors also match the organization's.

Recruiters used to be gatekeepers for the organization. Their task was to meet candidates, assess them, and make a shortlist of the ones they believed would be a good fit for the *organization* (and might be a good fit for the role). It was the hiring managers who then determined which candidate was the best fit for the *role*. What we found in our study, however, was that only 27% of recruiters are still interviewing candidates. The other 73% are just coordinating and shuffling requisitions.

So, if recruiters are no longer meeting candidates, who is assessing their organizational fit? The onus is now on hiring managers to not only fill their position but also ensure the candidate is the right fit for the organization. That creates a conflict of interest: do they hire the best person for the company, or do they hire a competent pair of hands to do the job today and worry about fit later? The most urgent problem for any hiring managers is the empty seat in their team area that needs filling. They have deadlines to meet and work piling up. They're not worried about whether a candidate has long-term potential: they just want to hire someone right now to get them through the next few months.

Dealing with that situation is primarily a matter of educating the hiring manager on the consequences of hiring someone who is a poor fit. While it may solve the problem in the short term, the new hire will probably only last a few months and then the manager will have to go through the process all over again. In that time, the manager will have disrupted the team to bring in a new person, invested time in training the new hire and getting them up to speed, and disrupted it again as that person leaves.

Fit Is About More Than Behaviors

We work with many high-tech companies with young, dynamic work-forces. Often, they'll have someone who was hired recently who is a little older and more experienced, and you can see that they feel like a fish out of water.

Many organizations use a standard set of interview questions for every role. Fit, if it's considered at all, is often assessed using behavioral-based questions to understand past experiences and behaviors, and the situations where the candidate worked well and where they didn't. The problem with that approach is that it assumes there is some set of characteristics that works across the board.

Fit doesn't just happen at the organizational level, however. There also has to be a match at the level of the team, division, and any other organizational units the new hire will belong to. It's easy to forget or ignore the importance of fit at those intermediate levels, but it can make the difference between hiring someone who stays and builds their career in the company and hiring someone who quits six months later.

Exit interviews repeatedly show that people join a company but leave a manager. In other words, they take a job in a company they feel aligned with, but then leave because they don't feel the same level of alignment with their team and their direct boss.

That's an expensive learning process for both sides. For the employee, it can set their career back by months or years, and for the company there are direct financial costs to replacing that employee. So, the hiring decision can't be based solely on whether someone will fit in at the organization. It has to take into account who they will be working for, and who will be working alongside them.

Within an organization, different subunits will have their own culture, and therefore their own factors that determine "fit"—just look at the Sales department in any company and compare it to the Finance function. Even though they are part of the same organization and they all fit with the company culture, most accountants would struggle to fit in with a team of sales people: their individual values, personalities, and profiles will be very different.

There may also be individual business units that don't fit the mold of the organization as a whole. For example, a company may have decided that the best fit culturally will be free-thinking creatives with a rebellious streak and a desire to stretch the boundaries of what is permitted. While those people may fit perfectly into 95% of jobs at the company, they may not be the right person for a regulatory compliance role.

The discussions may seem trivial at times—"This candidate is very religious, but he's going to be working with Michael who swears a lot"—but ignoring those factors can create unnecessarily tense situations. It's no longer enough to hire someone just because they can do the job well; there are too many other variables at play and they'll become disengaged if they're not the right fit for the organization.

"Fit" And Performance

It's hard if not impossible for someone to be a great performer if they're not also a great fit. That's why you can hire someone who was a top performer in their previous organization and even have them doing the same role, but if they don't fit, their performance will suffer. If a new hire isn't a good fit with their new organization's culture, values and environment, they are going to become frustrated and quickly lose motivation to perform above and beyond in the job. They will become disengaged and not enjoy the work they are doing. That, in turn, will impact other members of their team, potentially dragging those people down into disengagement or conflicts due to the difference in values.

The flipside to that is that you might hire someone who was a solid performer in their last company but not a superstar, and in the new environment they flourish and excel.

Fit is the secret sauce, the differentiator. You need to have a strong sense of why individuals succeed within the organization. There are many ways to assess that, ranging from conducting an extensive organizational assessment and audit to sitting down and thinking through what types of people have succeeded at your organization.

You can't do that based on gut feeling while sitting in an executive office: you have to ask the managers in the organization. When we work with our clients, for example, we'll ask "Who are the top performers on your team? What makes them a top performer? What do they bring to the table that makes them stand out?"

First, Know Yourself

As an organization, you can't hope to know whether someone will fit unless you first understand what your culture is. And you need to assess and reassess that regularly, because as you grow, things will shift.

We've worked with many startups that are typical dotcoms up to the point where they hit a hundred employees and the venture capitalists come in. That creates a major shift. Suddenly, the founders realize they need to act more "corporate"—especially from a compliance and regulatory side— and they bring in a COO who has a completely different approach from the founders.

As the company grows, accountabilities change. There are shareholders and investors, and you have to prove yourself to them constantly. That's when you realize that the earliest employees wouldn't be hired today. They wouldn't be a good fit for the company now that it has a thousand employees and it's listed on the stock exchange.

Sadly, those first hundred employees are usually still there but struggling. At one time, they might have overseen multiple divisions and had a lot of autonomy. You would think that those employees would move on of their own accord and find another startup or a more entrepreneurial company.

But experience shows that at least 20% of those original leaders choose to stay in their senior position.

Understanding the Environment

There is one major factor in fit has nothing to do with people: the work environment. For example, more and more organizations are taking down walls and creating open work areas with cubicles. That creates an environment where employees have no privacy. I've walked through many such buildings, and the hallways and washrooms are full of employees talking on cell phones, because that's the only place they feel comfortable making personal calls.

Some people thrive in that sort of environment. They enjoy having people around them. They love being able to turn to the person next to them to ask a question, to chat, to share a story or a joke, or whatever. Others hate the hubbub and the constant interruptions. They find it impossible to focus. They want somewhere quiet to sit and get on with their work. If someone has had a private office for the last five years, they're likely to struggle.

So, you need to be sure that a candidate is going to be able to work in their future environment. Make sure you interview them in a room just across from the team area and walk them through it, so they see what they're going to get into.

When Perks Become Stressors

One of our tech startup clients had grown rapidly to around a thousand employees. They hired us to look at their onboarding process, and as part of that work we spent time with both new hires and recent hires who had been there for some time.

While the company had been doing a great job of integrating new staff, virtually everyone we spoke to mentioned the stress they felt because of something that had been part of the culture of the company right from the start, when they were just a handful of people, and it had continued as the company expanded: "Beer Friday."

Every Friday afternoon, everyone would gather in the office and drink beer together. The problem was that the new hires were expected to buy the beer, and it was putting them under pressure. People were saying things like "I went to the store and I had no idea what to buy. I didn't want to look cheap, so I bought the most expensive beer I could find." Something that the company thought of as a perk and an icebreaker was in fact a source of stress and anxiety.

When we told leaders what was happening, they started buying the beer instead. They had never realized the tension it was causing, and nobody had ever told them.

It's Not Just About Fit

Every leader is different. They have their own personality, their own beliefs, their own behaviors. Some managers leave their team to get on with things, others are more hands on. Some expect their direct reports to come to them only once they finish the task, or if they hit a problem along the way; others want regular progress reports. Leadership style has a significant impact on engagement, and therefore on performance, so every leader is going to work well with a different profile of candidate.

While fit should always be a critical factor in hiring talent, it is not the only factor. You still need people with the proper skills, behaviors, etc. to do the job successfully. At the same time, you can't sacrifice "fit" when you hire—other factors such as experience, skills, etc. can be developed, but it is difficult to influence and change "fit" because that is about modifying someone's personality. So, the first thing to look for when searching for a great employee is somebody with a personality that fits with your company culture. One of the reflective questions I ask audiences in my keynotes is *Would you rather hire a young, smart person out of school and train them, or an experienced person?*

> *If you had to choose, which would you sacrifice when hiring?
> (source: Glassdoor 2017)*
>
> *a. Experience*
>
> *b. Skills*
>
> *c. Education*
>
> *d. Competencies*
>
> *e. Potential*
>
> *f. Fit*

Reflective Questions

How would you define your organization's culture? Does your current interview process assess a candidate's fit for your environment and culture?

Do your recruiters interview candidates for "fit" or are they simply pre-screening candidates to send to the hiring manager?

Do your hiring managers focus on candidates' long-term potential for your organization or are they hiring just to fill the position? Are they under pressure to fill open positions too quickly?

Do you know what makes top performers successful within your organization? How did your organization recognize the high potential in your top performers when they were candidates?

Are a candidate's "fit," skills, and experience seen as equally important? How would you rank the following in importance within hiring for your organization?

- Experience
- Skills
- Education
- Competencies/Behaviors
- Potential
- Fit

Do your hiring managers hire candidates based on their "gut feelings"?

How often do you speak with new hires about their experience during hiring and onboarding?

CHAPTER 3

Deskilled Hiring Managers

Over the last few years, organizations have cut back on training, education, and tools to prepare hiring managers to make good hiring decisions. As a result, candidates have a negative experience, the wrong people get into the organization, and expensive hiring mistakes happen.

The qualities of a good hiring manager are similar to those of a good leader: strong emotional intelligence, humility, and authenticity. Where a poor hiring manager will act as though the candidate is lucky to even be under consideration, a great hiring manager realizes they must continue to sell the opportunity to the candidate. In addition, from the recruiter's point of view, a good hiring manager is one who is collaborative and works well with everyone else involved in the hiring process.

Companies rarely review their hiring managers. If they did, they would find that, typically, at one extreme there are hiring managers who, either by experience or by natural disposition, are great at finding the best candidates and hiring them. These people need to be cultivated and encouraged to mentor others.

At the other extreme there are hiring managers who lack the communications skills, the interpersonal awareness, and the natural disposition to be great interviewers, and either don't care or don't want to do anything about it. Interestingly, those traits (or the lack of them) often reflect their effectiveness in other aspects of leadership.

Between those two endpoints lie the majority of hiring managers, who just need more experience and preparation. They are coachable and, for the most part, they want to do a great job of hiring. They just need support from the organization, from HR, and from hiring managers who excel.

When we train hiring managers for our clients, the first section of the one- or two-day workshop lays out the business case for great recruiting, and we rely on peer influence to bring that point home. We ask the client to mix up their best and worst hiring managers so that the room has a range of skill levels. That way, we can ensure the less-skilled hiring managers will get an "a ha" moment by the end of the training.

While the recruiter, as the one facilitating and managing the process, is the most important person in recruiting, the role of the hiring manager, as the ultimate decision maker, is critical. Whether it's a good hire or a bad one is down to them. You can be a great recruiter, with the best recruiting process in the world, but if you're dealing with a hiring manager who doesn't know what they want and is being difficult, you are never going to be successful.

The hiring manager is also, arguably, the architect of the candidate's experience. They are who the candidate will be working with, so they are the one the candidate wants to hear from and interact with. Whether or not the candidate accepts an offer is ultimately down to how well they connect with the hiring manager.

Hiring managers, however, rarely understand how pivotal their role is. Every organization has great leaders and poor leaders and it's usually the great leaders who get it and the poor leaders who just don't see how critical hiring is to not only their own success but also the organization's.

Interviewing Is A Skill That Has to Be Developed

The goal for every organization should be to develop all their hiring managers to be excellent at conducting interviews and selecting the right candidates. One of the best leaders I ever worked for used to tell business leaders "The decisions you make on who to hire will always be one of the most important business decisions you will make. So why wouldn't you want to be trained to make the best hiring decision you can?"

Given that most hiring managers are only recruiting once in a blue moon, how can they hone their skills and become excellent? As with any other skill, it is a matter of practice. Remember: candidates themselves will come to the interview better prepared than in the past. They have no qualms about practicing with a coach, anticipating the kinds of questions they may be asked, and planning their answers. Hiring managers need a similar level of preparation. They can no longer afford to just scan each candidate's résumé in the scant few minutes between interviews.

To help them, they can enlist colleagues or their recruiter to do mock interviews and go through the questions to figure out what they should be looking for and how to probe candidates' replies more effectively. Managers are often dismissive of role plays. And yet, they wouldn't hesitate to practice a critical presentation.

It's a matter of recognizing the importance and impact of recruitment. Every open position is an opportunity to make a difference, and to make an impact—positive or negative. You wouldn't allow a manager to walk into a meeting with a client or supplier unprepared, and you shouldn't tolerate hiring managers meeting a potential employee unprepared.

Buy-in on the importance of interviewing and hiring starts at the top and has to trickle down to all the leaders in the organization. Executives can reinforce the message by putting recruitment goals into every people leader's objectives. It needs to be tied to their rewards or bonus, and quantified and measured. That's the approach at fast-growing technology company PointClickCare, for example, who engaged us to build a hiring manager training module for their leadership development program. By making the training something that every leader goes through, the CEO is sending an unequivocal message that recruiting is vital to the company.

Beware of Hiring Clones

A significant risk in the recruitment process is the hiring manager who always hires in their own image. It's human nature for managers to seek out people who remind them of their younger self. In its most basic form, it can be as simple as always hiring graduates from their alma mater (often accompanied by actively rejecting candidates from schools that were their rival academically or on the sports field). It can also show up in the demographic or psychographic profile of the people a manager hires: favoring the candidate they could see themselves drinking beer with while watching the game, rather than the candidate who loves Wagner and took their last vacation in Austria visiting Mozart's birthplace.

Hiring clones creates many problems. Aside from diversity issues, it can be hard for anyone who doesn't fit "the profile" to integrate fully into the team, which exacerbates the problem over time. It's too easy to confuse connection (is this someone I'd personally love to work with?) and fit (is this someone who will thrive in this organization and role?), and to lose objectivity in the process.

The biggest compliment someone can pay you is when they walk into your office and say, "Wow, the diversity on your team is unbelievable." It would be easy for me to hire people for The Talent Company who love sports as much as I do, but I'd be missing out on a lot of great talent. I have a conscious mindset that says, "the candidate I click with best is not necessarily the one who will perform best in the job."

A great leader should always be looking for people who bring new ideas and new ways of doing things and will challenge the status quo. When you hire clones, there's a danger groupthink will set in. By hiring people just like you, you're adding people to the team without adding new perspectives. The people you bring in will probably think just like you, and they'll probably end up making the same decisions.

If you're wondering whether you've fallen into the 'cloning' trap (deliberately or accidentally), start by looking back at your hiring history. Who are the top performers you hired, and who are the duds? What was it about those top performers that made you hire them compared to what attracted you to the poor performers? That is real market data about what has worked for you and what hasn't.

Keeping It in The Family

Very similar to cloning is nepotism—hiring family and friends. While most people recognize that this can be a problem in small organizations where senior individuals can exert undue influence, it also happens in larger organizations that you might expect to be immune to it. In the corporate environment, it often extends beyond hiring, to managers deciding who gets a bonus and how much, who gets picked for promotion, who gets the best assignments or gets fast-tracked, and other management decisions.

It's hard to address performance challenges when the underperformer is your old school friend or to tackle the VP's nephew about his tardiness or attitude. If you do follow through and sack your friend, what happens to the friendship? And if you take the VP's nephew to task, how will your own performance review go?

Even if a friend or family member isn't being given preferential treatment, it can be difficult to overcome the perception that they have an advantage. So, you need to put in place policies and education to prevent nepotism from happening. While it's probably not feasible to have a blanket ban on hiring friends and family of existing staff—especially in a small town where everyone either knows or is related to everyone else—you can rule against setting up direct reporting lines between connected individuals and insist that anyone involved in the hiring decision declare conflicts of interest ahead of time and withdraw from the process.

There's No Such Thing as Unicorns

One of the biggest complaints I get from recruiters is that hiring managers keep asking them to find "unicorns"—a candidate profile (a list of skills and experiences required for a role) that simply does not exist in the labor market.

In our 2016 *Talent Acquisition Practices Study*, over 80% of the 155 talent acquisition leaders we surveyed felt that their hiring managers had unrealistic expectations about the required skills and experience for their open positions. At the same time, the 2016 *Job Seeker Nation Survey* by Jobvite—a yearly survey that analyzes the gaps between what hiring managers are looking for and what candidates are bringing to the table—found that only 7% of hiring managers said that "nearly all" or "most" job seekers had the right skills, character traits, and qualifications to fill open positions. In other words, 93% of hiring managers have unrealistic expectations.

That typically happens for one of three reasons. First, the combination of skills and experience may be so niche that it is virtually impossible to find in the market. Second, candidates with that profile might be common, but not at the level of pay and seniority offered. Third, candidates with that profile might be in high demand, so their pay expectations may be much higher than the position would normally justify.

> **93% of hiring managers have unrealistic expectations.**

Many hiring managers overvalue their position and its requirements, and they consider everything a must-have, making it impossible to find that skillset in the market. In that situation, the recruiter needs to get the hiring manager to prioritize: which of the requirements are truly a "must have," and which are simply "nice to haves"?

This doesn't just happen in white-collar jobs. As I was writing this book, I was preparing to give a keynote in a very industrial city in Ontario. One of the attendees emailed me in advance to ask if I could discuss the challenges of recruiting millwrights. Looking for millwrights is difficult everywhere, and part of the problem is that salary expectations have risen but companies haven't updated their pay offers to match. They still want to pay what they did two years ago, and candidates aren't interested.

Setting Realistic Hiring Timelines

Another common area of tension between hiring managers and recruiters is the time it will take to find and hire a candidate. From the hiring manager's perspective, their team member has just given two weeks' notice and they want continuity. In fact, they want the new person to start *before* the current employee leaves so that they can be trained.

The flaw in that idea should be obvious: whoever you hire is probably going to have to give notice to their current employer, too. Many people also want to take time off between jobs, so the timeline gets stretched further. And that's without taking into account the time to post the ad, get responses, carry out interviews, and all the rest of the recruitment process.

Recruiters Are Losing Touch

In common with most markets, labor markets are changing more rapidly and with increasing volatility. As the demands placed on recruiters have evolved, organizations have been slow to keep up. Companies in the US have made strides to adapt. However, Canadian companies are lagging. Most hiring managers lack practical knowledge of the labor market or don't recognize changing labor market conditions. That's especially true when it comes to salary expectations, where the recruiter's own experience gets in the way of understanding how markets are shifting.

Many organizations still rely on salary surveys to guide their pay deci-sions. Those surveys are compiled from data that is usually at least a year out of date, and sometimes longer. That wouldn't have been a problem ten years ago, but with markets today moving so quickly, the data is irrelevant by the time you get it. Another problem with salary surveys is that they are based on what people are being paid in their current role. While that may not sound like a problem, very few candidates are willing to change em-ployer for an opportunity that pays them the same as their current role.

The final problem is that salary surveys benchmark average pay. That's fine if your aim is to recruit average candidates, but if you're seeking the best talent in the market, that will come with its own price tag. The result is that in hot or growing markets, relying on salary survey data can damage your prospects of hiring good talent.

It's not just pay expectations that are rising more quickly than they used to. So are expectations around perks and benefits. When I started my career in the 1990s, annual bonuses were something that only executives got. To-day, the base expectation in many industries is that even at lower grades there will be a 5% year-end bonus. But remember, I said that candidates aren't going to move for a worse or equivalent package. So, if someone is getting a 5% bonus in their current role, they'll probably be looking for 10% in the next.

If salary surveys aren't reliable, then, how do we get more realistic data in advance? The worst approach is to wait for candidates to tell us we are being unrealistic. If you make ten offers and they all get rejected, it's a good indicator that you weren't in line with market expectations. In finding that out, however, you've burned your ten best candidates—the ones you liked so much that you made them offers—and your next offer is going to be to the person who, technically, was your eleventh choice.

A simple and less costly way would be to ask the candidate. The question to ask, however, is not the one most interviewers ask ("What are you currently making?") for the reason I explained above, but rather "What will it take to get you to move?" Another is to reach out to your professional network, whether in the 'real world' or online (for example on LinkedIn).

It's also important to assess your standing in the market realistically. If your company is seen as a "B" team in your market, think seriously about whether it's worthwhile trying to put together a package to attract "A" players, and whether you'll be able to keep them if you succeed. Even if you manage to hire them, there are two big risks. First, if a company that's bigger, better-known, and more coveted makes them an offer, they'll jump ship. Second, even if they don't get a competing offer, if they join your company and realize that they're not working on the kind of projects they were expecting, and that their new colleagues aren't at their level, they're going to start looking for new opportunities very quickly.

Market Data and Insights

Organizations struggle when hiring managers are focused on their immediate need, and recruiters aren't coaching or educating them in the realities of the market. A great recruiter who has a good relationship with the business may be comfortable setting realistic expectations, but recruiters who lack that connection and comfort are more likely to just say they are "on it" and set themselves up to fail.

Whenever a hiring manager brings a recruiter a new opportunity, the recruiter should be doing basic background research that will allow them to have a data-driven discussion about what they've found in the market. For example, hiring managers' ideas of what it will take in terms of salary and benefits to attract a good candidate are often out of date. When their recruiter pushes back and tells them they need to budget more, it's usually not well received. However, that conversation becomes easier if the recruiter can back it up with real market data. So, as part of their initial research, the recruiter should be looking for three top-level candidates and talking to them frankly about salary expectations. The responses will probably come as a shock to the hiring manager but will give them a realistic idea of what they need to pay.

The problem, of course, is that recruiters are already overextended. As I noted above, they are typically handling anything from 30 to 40 open requisitions at a time—and I've seen organizations where recruiters were juggling as many as eighty positions simultaneously. As a result, they don't have the bandwidth to do adequate research for every requisition.

How Organizations Respond

If you want high quality, focused recruiting, a recruiter's workload should be between 10 and 15 open positions. Above that, it's hard for them to give each requisition the attention it needs. We've already seen that the cost of hiring recruiters is rising, however. So, growing the Recruitment team to deal with demand is too expensive. The alternative is to reduce the number of open positions. But how do you do that in practice?

The first way is by reducing employee turnover. That starts with understanding why positions are becoming available. Sometimes it's due to growth, or because staff are moving up and their role has to be backfilled. Those are good reasons. But, of course, positions also open up when people leave. "A job for life" is long gone, and with it so is employee loyalty: people are more open to new opportunities, and they are more likely to be thinking about their next role even if they are happy in their current one. If you have great talent in roles, you need to make sure they stay there. So, you must pay attention to employee engagement and talent retention. In my presentations, I make the same point every time: do everything in your power to keep your top talent, because it's harder and more expensive to find new talent than to keep what you already have.

The second way to reduce recruiter workload is to prioritize between positions: for example, decide which are the top 50 critical open positions in the organization. Recruiters then focus on those and fill them before moving onto the other roles. The risk, of course, is that hiring managers will feel that their needs are being ignored. So, in Part Three we'll discuss how to do this without disengaging the hiring managers.

Recruiters Must Be Coaches

In recent years, many organizations have been switching from a transactional generalist model of HR to a Business Partner model where HR specialists act as coaches to the business. As part of that transformation, leading organizations typically align recruiters by skillset. For example, there might be a recruiter tasked with hiring marketers, another specializing in finance and accounting, etc.

Because those recruiters are hiring a specific kind of talent regularly, they are able to build a pipeline of candidates in their market and develop a deeper and more current understanding of the realities of the market than the hiring managers they work with, who may only be recruiting once or twice a year. That depth of knowledge and experience makes it easier to discuss priorities with a hiring manager when presented with a new requisition. The specialist recruiter can talk with authority about what they are seeing in the market and what they have observed in candidates for similar roles, and they can help the hiring manager adjust their desired candidate profile.

There are still, however, many organizations where recruiters prefer to be experts on hiring rather than on the disciplines they hire, and they would rather attend an HR conference than an industry event in their target field.

It's easy to understand why many companies—and their recruiters—haven't made that change. When a recruiter is handling 40 to 50 open roles, those positions are unlikely to all be in a single area, unless they're working for a major corporation. So, specialization becomes a nice-to-have.

Even when organizations do switch to the Business Partner model, however, they often will simply take someone who was a previously a generalist and give them a new business card that says *HR Business Partner*. Unfortunately, only a small percentage of recruiters have an innate ability to coach their hiring managers. Most aren't used to questioning authority. And, the less senior a recruiter is, the more likely they are to feel intimidated by a senior-level hiring manager who turns up with a list of demands, so they become order takers rather than coaching and influencing the manager.

One of the simplest ways to make recruiting more effective is, therefore, to have better recruiters. Too often, when I go into a company and assess their recruitment practices, CHROs are blaming the recruiters for any hiring problems. In at least 75% of the organizations I work with, however, the recruiters have been set up to fail. They have the capability, but they aren't given the opportunity to shine. They are dealing with too many open positions, with systems that aren't set up to support them, working to unrealistic requisitions from the hiring managers. So, even if they have the skills to coach and influence, they don't have the time to do it.

The Three Directions of Hiring Managers

Best-in-class organizations recognize the importance of investing in their hiring managers' recruitment and interviewing capabilities through ongoing education and tools. These organizations guide their hiring managers in one or more of three directions—based on their personality, experience, and personal preferences—and train them appropriately:

1. Talent scouts
2. Talent ambassadors
3. Talent assessors

Talent Scouts focus on networking and driving referrals. They have a mindset that says *If I come across great people in my day-to-day life, I want to engage them and tell them about our organization.* If they meet someone who matches what they're looking for—whatever the circumstances—they'll find a way to start the conversation, whether it's giving their card to the server who gave them great service at a restaurant, or a phone call to the person who sat next to them at a conference and impressed them with their knowledge.

Talent Ambassadors focus on their personal impact on the overall candidate experience. That may be at the individual level (by being prepared for interviews and engaging candidates), or organizationally (by driving improvements to the recruitment process).

Talent Assessors focus on their role as a gatekeeper responsible for selecting the right talent for their organization. They are highly skilled at understanding people.

Very few leaders are strong in all three areas, so there's an opportunity for recruiters to leverage the relative strengths of individual hiring managers by allowing them to specialize in the aspects of recruiting that play to their strengths rather than forcing them into roles they're less comfortable with.

Recruitment training and leadership programs rely on self-awareness. The more a hiring manager understands which aspects of hiring they are good at—and which not—the better they will do, and the more likely they are to reach out for help to peers who they know are strong in complementary areas. The final hiring decision will still be theirs, but they will come to it with more insight and evidence.

> *Here are some self-awareness questions I encourage hiring managers to consider:*
>
> - *Am I an engaging person, or am I someone who gives long answers and talks all the time?*
> - *Am I a good listener?*
> - *Do I encourage candidates to ask me questions?*
> - *Am I intimidating to candidates?*

Getting Managers Engaged

Whatever training you offer your hiring managers has to be tailored and customized for your organization. Many training companies can provide off-the-shelf programs, but those will often turn hiring managers off rather than energizing them. It can be something as simple as the language the trainer uses: referring to "the company" when the organization is a professional service firm or talking about "profit" in a government department.

In designing bespoke programs for many clients, we've found that managers have to see value in the training program. It has to be driven by tangible recruitment objectives that address the organization's specific hiring challenges, whether that be improved candidate assessment in interviews, turning hiring managers into talent ambassadors, getting better at closing candidates, or something else.

Another critical success factor we've discovered is the power of co-facilitating trainings with a member of the organization's own HR or recruitment teams and bringing recruiters into the training sessions alongside hiring managers so they can build relationships. That also allows recruiters to play the candidate in mock interviews with the hiring managers—another opportunity to create rapport and move away from an "us and them" mindset. Recruiters and hiring managers then become joint stakeholders in making the organization successful.

Finally, training can't be a single event; there have to be ongoing opportunities to refresh and reengage with the content, and to receive coaching.

Reflective Questions

What percentage of your hiring managers truly understand the importance of their role in hiring great talent for your organization?

Do your hiring managers know what defines a "great" candidate for your organization?

How prepared are your hiring managers for interviewing and hiring candidates? Do you offer your hiring managers training on interviewing, candidate experience, and making hiring decisions?

Are your hiring managers evaluated for their interviewing and hiring performance? Are they recognized and rewarded for their success?

Do your recruiters/HR business partners act as recruitment and hiring coaches to your hiring managers?

Do your recruiters understand the current labor market and the changing conditions?

Is your organization able to attract and engage top talent in the market? How competitive are your organization's current salaries and total compensation packages?

On average, how many open requisitions do your recruiters work on at a time?

Do your hiring managers see recruitment and hiring as an HR responsibility or as part of their responsibilities?

CHAPTER 4

Increasing Reliance on Technology

From Applicant Tracking Systems to assessments, organizations are placing increasing reliance on technology to drive recruitment, investing millions of dollars in the hope that it will solve their recruitment challenges. Instead of supporting the recruitment process, however, technology is being allowed to drive it. Machines decide who you interview, who you reject, and who goes forward at each stage. Unfortunately, computers are screening out good candidates before they've even had a conversation. That damages the candidate experience and robs you of potential talent.

Every time a new technology hits the recruitment market, it's positioned as the solution to all your problems. When applicant tracking systems (ATSs) were launched in the late 1990s/early 2000s, the promise was that you wouldn't even need human recruiters any more. This miraculous system would post your jobs, and applicants would magically find your website, spend an hour completing an online application and adding their résumé, and you would have all the information you needed to select your perfect candidate.

Then, in the late 2000s/early 2010s, candidate assessment systems started to appear. This time the promise was that if you bought the software, you would never again make a bad hire. Coupled with the idea that ATSs will give them the best candidates to put through those assessments, it's an enticing proposition.

Both premises show a frightening lack of understanding of the role—and value—of human recruiters. It's a deeply transactional approach, driven by an underlying assumption that all a recruiter does is collate and preselect résumés.

It's interesting going into organizations that have been investing heavily in those technologies. Often, the majority of their recruitment budget is being spent on software and systems. When those organizations ask me for one thing they can do to move the needle in their recruiting, my answer is the same as in the last chapter: hire great recruiters.

Recruiters rave about how much data they can get about potential candidates from LinkedIn and Facebook, but the reality is they often have far more information in their own database already. Back in 2006, I met with the head of Talent Acquisition of a major international retailer. Their database held the contact details of over one million candidates who had applied for past roles. The only problem was, none of them were being contacted. Whenever a new position became available, the recruiters would post it publicly without even thinking to look at who was already in the system. The company had the opportunity to engage a million candidates, but they were ignoring it.

Systems are useful for managing and organizing the recruitment process. By putting all the applications and résumés you receive into a database, they help you to search and manage those applications in ways that were impossible in the days of paper-based records. The problem with that is that— like the retailer above—most organizations that have had an ATS for the last 15 years probably have over a million people in their database, but they never go back to any of them. So, every time they need to hire someone, they start from scratch, posting the job and seeing who applies.

It's much easier to post a new ad and get 300 fresh applicants than to search a database of millions of names, especially since some of those applicants may be from a long time ago and you need to qualify their current interest level. Some recruiters may be happy picking up the phone and restarting the conversation—and getting a lot of rejections—but many recruiters would rather talk only to new applicants who they know are interested.

It's Not All Doom and Gloom

Despite the dismal picture I just painted of recruiting technologies, there are some excellent systems on the market that are marketed as Candidate Relationship Management software.

I said earlier that recruiters need to think and behave like sales professionals. Candidate relationship management systems apply the principles of a sales Customer Relationship Management system to the recruitment cycle. The problem is that if a company has invested heavily in an ATS, they're not going to abandon that for a candidate relationship management system. So, until ATS vendors develop better candidate relationship management modules, those companies probably aren't going to implement candidate relationship management.

Recruitment Is A Human Process

When you ask candidates what their biggest issue is with recruitment, it's the lack of human touchpoints in the hiring process. Candidates want—and need—to speak to real people. They don't want to be "automated" and have a computer tell them they aren't right for the role. If they've applied, they have invested in your brand and they are interested in working for you. That alone should earn them at least a little respect. Sending a stream of form emails that start "Dear candidate" shows no respect and will ultimately impact your consumer brand and your employer brand negatively.

That said, up to 64% of candidates never hear back at all from an organization after applying for a job[3]. All it would take to solve that is one simple

---

[33] CareerBuilder survey 2017

automated email, but for some reason organizations don't even set that up in their systems. I'd like to think it's because they realize that it should be a human getting in touch. Unfortunately, it's more likely to be that the recruiters don't have the time or that they don't understand the full functionality of the system. They may not even realize that there is an option to set up an automated response.

So, just as our education platform client discovered, applicants submit their résumé and they have no idea what's happening. In the meantime, they may also have applied for other roles, and if your competitor responds but you don't, they'll probably take the job with your competitor—even if they wanted to work for you and the other job was just a safety net.

People Are the Block

Part of the reason why technology can't fix a broken recruiting process is that the same people are still running it. Too many organizations spend money on recruitment technologies and assume that everything will be good from that point on. In order to fix the process, however, you have to change the recruiters' behaviors. They are the ones who have to drive improvement and become proactive in pipelining, candidate relationship management, candidate nurturing, and building talent communities.

The plain truth is, if your Recruitment function isn't working properly with humans driving it, technology won't make it work better. The real value comes in building processes that work, managed by a successful team, and adding technology systems to support them.

One Size Does Not Fit All

The implementation of any system has to be tailored to the organization and its needs. Every organization is different, and one size never fits all.

When I joined American Express, I had the opportunity to work with many countries around the world to build their recruitment capability. The biggest frustration every time was the applicant tracking system. The technology was part of a broader global decision-making process, and it created some situations which would be comical if they weren't so aggravating.

For example, there was a standard question we asked every candidate in the online application, "How did you hear about this opportunity?" and they would pick a response from a dropdown list. Rather than customizing the list to the local market, however, the system displayed every media outlet and website where jobs were being posted anywhere in the world. Candidates had to scroll through over a hundred menu items, and they would be sitting in Toronto, wondering why we were asking if they'd seen the ad in the Australian Financial Review. Inevitably, candidates just picked something that started with an A and we got no useful data from the exercise.

Building A One-Stop Shop

Many vendors are trying to develop a single platform that combines the functionality of all the HR and recruiting systems in the same way that ERP systems have consolidated business process management. Unfortunately, no single platform has yet managed to integrate everything—they all have gaps—and on the whole, none of the systems currently available are as good at any of the individual functions as the best dedicated tools on the market.

Of course, it would be difficult to create an all-singing, all-dancing system that provides best-in-class functionality for every step of the recruitment journey for every organization. For example, assume you're a recruiter who has compiled a list of two hundred potential candidates and now you want to find out their email address so you can contact and engage them.

In principle, that functionality should be available in your Recruitment platform. In practice, however, Recruitment is just one package within the HR module of the broader corporate information system, and it's not considered core functionality by vendors or, indeed, by organizational IT buyers, so adding specialized functionality like email search isn't top of their list. Instead, you have to rely on standalone tools like emailhunter.com that allow you to enter the profile of someone you're looking for and they will find an email address. That isn't going to change until more organizations make recruitment a strategic priority.

Should Assessments be Automated?

Another area where technology is widely used in recruitment is assessment. While assessing candidates is essential—and a key step in the model I present in Part Two of this book—the execution of that assessment often leaves a lot to be desired. Part of the challenge is making sure that the people carrying out assessments are properly trained. A bigger problem, however, is that in trying to address that challenge, organizations have turned to technology—automated assessment tools—and created even bigger problems in turn.

For an HR director trying to lighten the workload of recruiters and hiring managers, putting a candidate through a battery of online personality tests and psychometric assessments feels proactive. It feels like they're finally screening for fit without having to waste time with unsuitable candidates.

The problem is, it doesn't work.

The Candidate Perspective

If we put ourselves in the candidate's shoes and look at automated assessments, a poorly designed or executed assessment process creates a negative impression that can be a major dissatisfier. Organizations make the problem worse by mismanaging candidates' expectations. I've known candidates who were halfway through a recruitment process when the company suddenly asked them to come in for an assessment. They turned up expecting a thirty-minute test and instead found themselves in a four-hour assessment center.

In addition, some assessments are poorly written, with questions that are potentially highly offensive, clumsy questions that are blatantly testing your integrity, or pointed questions that make you wonder how anyone would dare ask that. It's like the immigration forms that ask *Have you ever been a terrorist? Have you ever plotted to overthrow the government?* No one has ever answered *Yes*.

Even if the assessment experience is positive, however, it won't achieve the objective, for one very simple reason. In any other situation, if you put people through an assessment, they will approach it as an opportunity to learn about themselves. They take time to reflect, be honest with themselves, and answer truthfully. But this isn't any other situation. It's a recruitment process, and the candidate wants the job. So instead of sitting down thinking *Let's find out who I am*, they are thinking *Who do I need to be to get this job?*

The Organizational Perspective

Part of the problem is that organizations misuse assessment platforms in much the same way that they misuse other recruitment technologies. Many companies use automated assessments as the primary decision-making mechanism for candidate selection or advancement. They'll ask a candidate to attend three or four interviews, then put them through an assessment. If the candidate's results are bad, it doesn't matter how many human interviewers said the candidate was good—the computer says *No*, so they're out.

Assessment tools can be used to gain greater insight into candidates, but there has to be an interview to validate the findings of the assessments. We guide our clients towards assessments that can make human interviews richer; that suggest specific questions to ask a candidate based on their results or areas to focus on in the conversation. They're a support for the human recruiter, not a substitute.

The Right Assessment for The Right Job

Many organizations have a standard battery of tests that every candidate has to take, whether they're applying for a job in the mail room or the C-suite. In those situations, a candidate could easily be asked to take a test that has no bearing on their ability to do the job they've applied for. And yet, if they fail it they are eliminated from consideration.

For example, it's one thing to ask a potential executive assistant to take test of their PowerPoint and Word skills. It's quite another to ask a sales director to take those tests. However, if your recruiting systems are set up with a single standard assessment process—as many are—that's exactly what will happen. And your potential sales director may start to wonder what the job really entails if they're being tested on how well they know Office.

Psychologists Don't Help

Many organizations still use industrial psychologists to put candidates through a range of assessments, paying anything from $5,000 to $10,000. The problem comes when the recruiter and hiring manager turn the psychologist into the decision maker. It's another manifestation of the lack of conviction and confidence hiring managers feel in making a recruitment decision. They want someone else to tell them what to do and who to hire.

Buyer Beware

Assessment vendors sell on fear—the fear of hiring the wrong person, or missing the right one—and each year, organizations spend millions on acquiring the latest assessment tools, pitched to them as the solution for all their hiring problems.

The problem is, every organization has its own culture and environment, and the characteristics that make someone successful in one company could make them fail in another. By the same token, every organization has its own unique definition of what makes a "great" candidate. Even within a single organization, the criteria for success will be different for different roles: what makes someone a top sales person will not be the same qualities that make someone a top engineer.

So, any assessment tool you use has to be customized for your organization, your department, your team, and even for individual roles. Out of the box, however, most assessment tools aren't versatile enough to take into account an organization's unique needs.

Using Assessments Properly

Making proper use of assessments in recruitment starts with understanding why you are introducing those assessments—the specific challenges or gaps you are trying to address. That will determine not only what assessments you introduce, but also how, and allow you to tailor the assessments not just to the organization but also to the objective. For example, if you've identified organizational fit as a problem area in hiring, then the assessment vendor will need to come in and understand the company culture so that they can build a customized assessment.

Once you understand what you're trying to achieve or fix, you need to decide where in the process the assessment should happen. Timing is critical. If you introduce assessments too soon, you're probably using them to screen applicants.

Some organizations build the assessment into the application process on their applicant tracking system, so if they get 300 applicants for a job, all 300 people complete the test. In that list, however, there might only be two or three candidates who are qualified for the job. Testing all 300 is a colossal waste of money that could be avoided with a simple preliminary screening step administered by a human recruiter. There are also low-cost ($10-$500) online assessments that can be introduced early in the process to assist with screening so that you only put people forward for more expensive assessments—or an assessment center run by professional assessors and psychologists—once they make the shortlist.

At the other extreme, there are companies that use assessments in the final stages of the recruitment process, once they've settled on their chosen candidate (and declined all the others). If the assessment results come back negative, however, they're back at the start of the process but they've turned away a lot of good potential hires along the way.

Assessment Centers

When you're building assessments into your process, thinking from a candidate perspective goes a long way. If you put in a battery of assessments, you risk putting giving off candidates a poor experience, and some good may pull out of the process altogether. There's also a risk that you'll reject a great candidate simply because they scored poorly on an assessment.

Sometimes, organizations condense all their assessments into an assessment center where candidates can be put through their paces in a block. The exact combination of assessments used will depend on the role and seniority being recruited, but it often includes personality assessments alongside case studies, aptitude tests, and assessments of specific skillsets.

These assessment centers are a valuable part of recruitment at junior levels—I've often used them in campus recruiting. When it comes to C-level roles, however, they can be more of a problem than a solution. I've even seen organizations that send every senior level candidate to an indus-trial psychologist for a half-day or full-day training—it's an expensive exer-cise for the company and a major imposition on candidates.

For example, we worked with an organization that had engaged a third-party firm to run five-hour assessment centers. When we spoke to candi-dates who had been through that process, the feedback we got consistently was that they had completely disengaged with the organization afterward. Indeed, it was such a bad experience that most of them pulled out of the process altogether.

The Positive Impact of Technology

By now, it sounds like I'm a luddite who hates technology and thinks it has no role in recruitment and talent acquisition. Nothing could be further from the truth. Used properly, technology has incomparable power and po-tential to make recruitment faster, simpler, and cheaper.

Technology—especially social media—connects recruiters to virtually anyone they need to find and creates a path of communication. It also gives employers more control over their brand than ever before. At its simplest, that might be just a careers site with a list of open positions, and infor-mation about what it's like to work for the organization. More proactive organizations build up that presence with videos of real employees—not actors—talking about their experience. Those videos can then be posted not only on the careers site, but across social media platforms.

Technology gives employers more control over their brand than ever before.

Glassdoor Is A Goldmine

One aspect of their brand that companies can't control, however, is what gets posted on review sites. Earlier, I discussed how Glassdoor—the market leader in that space—can give candidates insider insights into an organization, but recruiters can benefit from the site too. When I'm delivering a keynote or a seminar, I usually ask the audience whether they know Glassdoor and whether they are using it. The interesting thing is that when I ask CFOs or other C-level executives, as many as half the audience say yes. If I put the same question to an audience of HR professionals, however, only one in four will put their hand up. In other words, general executives are more comfortable with Glassdoor than HR managers. That's shocking. Almost as shocking as watching a room full of recruiters and HR people manically scribble down the URL so they can go back to their office and check it out.

Every person working in recruitment in your organization—every recruiter, every HR manager and HR partner, and every hiring manager—should at least be logging into Glassdoor and seeing what people are saying about you. When we run recruitment workshops for hiring managers, one of the first things we get them to do is to go to the company's page on Glassdoor and see what their candidates and employees have written. We were running one such workshop for a mining company last year and brought up their Glassdoor page. An employee had written "Great place to work but the men's bathrooms at this mine are disgusting." The HR person at the back of the room was horrified. Meanwhile, the hiring managers were all nodding. They knew it was a problem, but no-one had ever thought to tell HR.

The great thing about technology is that it gives you access to that sort of feedback: things that the people who work for you might never think to bring to management's attention but can make their life easier or more pleasant.

Glassdoor also tells you how candidates perceive your organization. For example, they can post the questions they were asked at interview and what they thought of the whole experience. When you're trying to improve the candidate experience, that kind of feedback is priceless—and something that you would never get by asking candidates directly, especially if you've just told them they won't be going forward. Having that information in the public domain may seem like a problem, but that's only the case if your interviewers are merely working their way through a static checklist of questions. If, on the other hand, your interviewers are trained to dig deeper—to probe and verify the answers—then it can actually be beneficial if candidates know what they will be asked, because they'll come prepared with their best answers. But, you do have to be certain that your interviewers are skilled enough to get to the truth.

Of course, Glassdoor isn't just about you: it's also about your competitors. So, you can use the site to find out what they are doing too. You could, for example, identify the pain points candidates have in their recruitment processes and use that knowledge to poach the best candidates away from them. If that sounds familiar, it's because it's the way your peers in sales and marketing are already using social media and consumer reviews sites.

Where Next?

LinkedIn transformed the way companies reach candidates. Not too long ago, recruitment was driven by large job aggregator boards like Monster, Indeed, and Career Builder. If you wanted access to candidates, that's where you posted your job. As demand rose, the boards raised their fees, and companies started to look for an alternative. That opened up a massive opportunity for LinkedIn, and they turned it into a significant revenue stream. In fact, the company's steady income from recruitment was a major factor that led to its acquisition by Microsoft. The problem with using LinkedIn for recruitment, however, is that people typically only get active on there when they start looking for a job. If someone is happy in their role, they may have a profile, but it probably won't have been updated in a couple of years and they're too busy to log on regularly. So, the big question for recruiters is *What's next? What's the new LinkedIn?* Let's look at four key technologies: Twitter, pay per click, mobile, and SMS.

Twitter: Many recruiters try to use Twitter for recruitment, but people generally aren't looking for a job when they're on the site. So, even if you post an ad, your candidates probably won't see it.

Pay per click: Online advertising is becoming far more personal and targeted, and that is the most likely direction that recruitment technology will take: a 180-degree turn away from traditional "post and pray" advertising towards more personalization and more customization. If you can get your ad in front of a much smaller but highly targeted audience, then your chances of getting the right candidate to apply increase exponentially even though there are fewer eyeballs on your ad. When it comes to personalization in advertising, the two major players are Facebook and Google, and the next big shift in recruitment technology is likely to come from them.

While people tend to think of LinkedIn as "the professional networking site" and Facebook as "the social network," the reality is that, regardless of whether it's for personal reasons or professional, Facebook is where many people are spending an increasing proportion of their time every day. For recruiters, Facebook is an untapped market, and its developers have been watching what works on LinkedIn and creating recruitment-centric tools.

Google has also been working on a set of tools for corporate recruiters and is investing heavily in different apps for organizations and for candidates.

Mobile: Mobile technologies are also becoming increasingly important. Sitting at your desk in a corporate office, it's easy to assume that the world consumes the internet on a laptop screen. However, the majority of web browsing today takes place on smartphones. That's a problem for recruiters, because only 40% of company career sites are optimized for mobile viewing, and even fewer make it possible for someone to apply for a job on a smartphone.

SMS: Increasingly, I hear recruiters complain that they leave voicemails for candidates, but no one ever replies. That's because candidates, especially younger ones, would rather get a text message. They don't check their mobile voicemail regularly and they probably never log into their office voicemail inbox at all. Of course, an older recruiter who only ever gets texts from friends and family may feel uncomfortable texting a candidate, but if that's what they want, then you need to adapt.

On the plus side, text messaging forces you to be brief, which is an advantage. Most candidates don't want a lengthy job description. They just want the value proposition and the opportunity spelt out briefly.

Catching Up

Despite all the downsides I identified in this chapter, technology has had and can have a very positive impact on recruitment. Technology gives recruiters direct access to the best candidates, and the means to identify them. It gives recruiters valuable insight into the candidate experience, how the organization is truly seen in the employment market, and what its competitors are doing. When used correctly, in other words, technology is an essential source of competitive advantage in the employment market.

Talent acquisition professionals love to find out what other organizations are doing and then try it out in their own company. Unfortunately, following trends blindly and doing what all the other companies in your industry are doing isn't going to make you stand out as a great employer to candidates.

Too many companies are afraid to try anything truly new and innovative. There's an overwhelming sense of inertia. As a result, a lot of the technical innovation in recruitment is coming from fast-growing technology companies that both have the money to invest in new technologies and understand the need for great talent. Rather than focusing purely on technology, however, organizations need to think more broadly about how to innovate in talent acquisition. They should be looking for new programs and practices that will differentiate them in the market.

Reflective Questions

How much of your budget for recruitment and hiring is spent on technology applications?

How is technology used in screening applicants or candidates? Does technology play a positive or negative role in your current recruitment and hiring process?

In what ways does your current applicant tracking system improve your hiring process? Do your recruiters consider past applicants and candidates already in the applicant tracking database?

Do all applicants hear from your organization after applying for a role? Are there enough "human touchpoints" with applicants and candidates in your hiring process?

Do you set expectations early enough with candidates around what to expect during the hiring process?

How positive an experience for candidates is the assessment phase of your hiring process? How effective are your candidate assessments? Have you measured their real impact on your hiring process?

Are assessments used to provide additional insights into candidates or are they being used to make hiring decisions? Are insights from hiring assessments used to inform the new employee's onboarding and development planning?

How effective is your recruitment and employer branding on social media?

Is your organization using mobile technology effectively in the recruitment and hiring process?

CHAPTER 5

Employer Branding Is Giving Way to Peer Reviews

The old mindset of hiring a recruitment marketing firm to build your employer brand and write your employment ads has been superseded by online platforms like Glassdoor, where candidates and employees alike share their experiences—good, bad and downright ugly—with the world. Sadly, many employers still fail to recognize this feedback or to do anything with the insight it provides into how they are seen by the outside world.

One of our clients is a high-tech healthcare company that has been around for over fifteen years. They were struggling to hire the people they wanted, so the first piece of work we did for them was a talent acquisition assessment. It soon became clear that candidates didn't see them as somewhere they would want to work—not because it was a bad place to work, but because they had a very weak employer brand which was making it hard for them to attract A-list candidates, especially as they were in direct competition with big-name technology companies for the best talent.

They had an excellent reputation among their target customers but no one else was aware of them: if you drove past their offices, you would have no idea who they were unless you were in procurement in the healthcare industry. Interestingly, though, when candidates did come in for interview, they became engaged and enthusiastic as soon as they were in the building and talking to people—but we had to get them through the door first.

The company had an amazing story to tell about how it started and the products and services it delivers, but that story wasn't getting told. So, the solution was to tell it. We created videos to tell the story, we helped current employees to understand their role as brand ambassadors, and we created a referral campaign: all strategies that you'll learn about in Part Three, when we discuss sourcing and pipelining. As a result, over the last two years the company has become a "destination" employer: a company that people specifically want to work for, on a par with major consumer-facing tech brands.

Employer Brands and Recruitment Brands: What's the Difference? (And Why Should You Care?)

An organization's recruitment brand is a subset of its overall employer brand. Where the employer brand represents the market's perception of what it's like to work for the organization, the recruitment brand is about the kinds of candidates and skillsets it is looking for.

While an organization may have overall corporate employer and recruitment brands, individual business units often have their own brands ("I've heard that working in technology sales at that organization is a nightmare," or "I've heard that the finance department at that company is implementing a radical new budgeting approach."). That allows recruiters and hiring managers to create highly targeted messages, tailored to their ideal candidates—and potentially even to a specific individual—that speak to what matters most to the candidate and show them why they need to work for the company rather than any other employer.

To do that, recruiters and hiring managers need to know their target candidates very well. Imagine you are a recruiter looking for JAVA programmers. As you start to do your research, you discover that, while they attach some significance to salary and benefits, they are much more likely to be motivated by the type of projects they'll be involved in. When recruiting those programmers, you might emphasize the cutting-edge work they'll be doing. For recruits in other areas, however, the message will be different.

The Yelpification of Recruitment

The most important thing you can do in creating your recruitment brand is to be authentic. Don't claim you're a "green" company that cares for the environment when your executives are driving gas-guzzling trucks or big-engined sports cars. That starts with self-awareness at the organizational level: *What are we good at? Why do people work here? What are the challenges? What are the opportunities?*

When I'm giving a keynote, I'll put up two photographs of hotel rooms. One is a 5-star suite at the Four Seasons, the other is a dive motel. The old model was to promote your business as the equivalent of the Four Seasons, even if in reality you were the roach motel. In the world of Facebook and Glassdoor, companies can't get away with that anymore. The voice of candidates is loud and clear in the market, and so is the voice of new employees who come in and realize that the organization they've joined is not what they'd expected.

The upside is that, as we saw earlier, sites like Glassdoor give organizations access to the minds of candidates and employees alike. In ways that our predecessors could never have imagined, today's recruiters and hiring managers need to listen and engage with a candidate. When they do that, they can be honest about not only what's great about a role, but also the challenges.

Curating the Recruitment Brand

A company's recruitment brand—and its employer brand also—have to be authentic and realistic. Fortunately, it's easier than ever to create authentic video. Gone are the days when you needed to hire a professional production crew. Today, organizations are using videos on their websites that have been filmed with a smartphone: real employees walking through a real building sharing real thoughts about what it's like to work there and what to expect.

In my early career, employer and recruitment brands were typically built by an external recruitment marketing firm and the work usually resulted in an ad campaign that represented how the company wanted to be perceived rather than communicating the reality of working there. The assumption was that, once someone started working for the company, they would probably stay even if the reality didn't match up to the promises. One of the companies I worked for went so far as to hire professional actors to play employees talking about how much they enjoyed working there. Nowadays, it wouldn't get away with that.

"The employee voice is an essential piece of a company's employer brand."—Carmel Gavin, CHRO, Glassdoor.

As recently as 2010, I was at a conference where a group of HR leaders from the health industry were discussing whether they should ban employees from using LinkedIn completely, or just discourage them. Some were even debating whether employees should be allowed to access the internet at all while at work. Even if they don't take such extreme positions, many organizations still discourage employees from posting online feedback.

The employees who post on Glassdoor, however, are typically the ones who are disengaged or have performance challenges, and they aren't going to pay much attention to a company ban on posting reviews. A much smarter approach is to actively encourage top performers and committed employees to post feedback. That way, you drown out the negative voices of the disgruntled few with positive messages from people who enjoy working for you.

Creating or curating the organization's recruitment brand is not a leadership task. It is something that is best treated as a grassroots initiative led by talent ambassadors and involving all employees. One quick win can be to encourage *everyone* to see themselves as a talent ambassador: to understand the core message of why people should work there (or not), and to go out and talk to people who would fit in well. All of this assumes, of course, that the organization is one that people want to work for.

It's Not Just About the Money

Traditionally, organizations have focused on salary benefits to "sell" candidates on the idea of working there. That's only part of the deal, though: we are all looking for something different from a job or an employer. It's true that for many people salary and benefits are very important. But when a candidate is comparing similar offers from multiple organizations—especially if there is a "market rate" for their skillset—the decision stops being about compensation.

Some candidates will look at the type of work, the mission and vision of the organization, the people they met with at each stage of the recruitment process, public perceptions of the key executives and of the firm, and a wide range of other factors that the company can't control and will struggle to communicate. Other candidates may focus on social factors: what the company does to give back to the community, whether there are charity days or organized volunteering, or how environmentally conscious the organization is.

Because there are so many factors to consider, often the only people who can really convey all of those nuances are the people who work there. I've mentioned Glassdoor several times in this book. Glassdoor is just one—albeit the most popular—of a number of sites that have sprung up where candidates and employees can share what they really think about a company.

According to an October 2017 report by iCIMS, *The Modern Job Seeker*, 92% of jobseekers think employee reviews are an important factor when deciding whether to apply to a job. Of those, 37% consider those reviews to be the most important factor and nearly one in three candidates has turned down a job offer primarily because the company had negative online employer reviews. At the managerial level, the percentage is even higher: 43%.

In the future, smart organizations will stay ahead of this trend by making employees a core part of both the recruitment process and how they attract candidates, perhaps even giving candidates live access to current employees. Even though candidates may not know an employee personally, they will pay more attention to what they hear from someone who works at the company than anything they might read on the corporate website.

The Role of The Recruiter

In this process of curating the recruitment brand, the recruiter is conductor, coach, and advisor. While final accountability may rest with senior levels of the organization, the recruiter is the one coaching stakeholders in the hiring process, reinforcing the messaging, making sure that it stays realistic and authentic, and reminding them of the need to be selling candidates throughout the process.

The recruiter should also be ensuring that stakeholders remember that recruitment is a two-way conversation. Interviewers need to be prepared for probing questions from candidates: "Why do you like working here? What made you leave your past organization and come here? What keeps you engaged on a Sunday night? Why do you look forward to coming to work?" The recruiter can't script the answers to those questions, but they can coach each stakeholder to create their own responses. And, while the recruiter may help them polish the language, it's essential to keep the answers authentic and genuine.

Reflective Questions

How authentic is your recruitment and employer brand as portrayed in your recruitment ads and postings?

How do candidates view your organization in the market? Do you look at your organization's profile and posted feedback on Glassdoor on a regular basis?

What is your organization's candidate value proposition? How effective are your recruiters and hiring managers in articulating that candidate value proposition?

Who are your organization's competitors for talent in today's market? How is your candidate value proposition different from those talent competitors' proposition?

Why do candidates accept employment offers with your organization?

CHAPTER 6

The Candidate Experience

A negative candidate experience has an impact beyond the immediate role. Good candidates will walk away, and never come back, and everyone will tell or post to their friends about the way you treated them. That impacts not only your employer brand but potentially your consumer brand, too. Whether someone's experience is positive or negative, however, usually comes down to communication setting and expectation management.

We were engaged by a large technology company that works with mortgage appraisers and home inspectors. In the early days, the entire company consisted of 25 people working in a single office and the CEO had been able to meet every candidate in person before they were hired. Now that they had grown to 1,000 employees worldwide, however, the CEO was still insisting on meeting every potential new hire personally. It had become a serious bottleneck in the recruitment process, and urgent hiring decisions were being delayed because the CEO didn't have time in his schedule.

The bigger problem, however, was that the CEO himself was someone candidates either loved or hated, and half of the people who got an offer would decline it. Candidates who had been enthusiastic throughout the interview process were being turned off either by the hassle of trying to schedule time with the CEO or because they didn't get on with him in the meeting even though they might never have to interact with him in the course of their work.

To remedy the situation, we replaced the CEO interview with a screening and closing meeting with the Senior Vice President of HR. Hiring timelines shortened dramatically, and the proportion of offers accepted increased.

One of my biggest complaints about recruiting is the lack of respect given to candidates throughout the recruitment process. Whether it be a poor recruiter behaving in a way that doesn't respect the candidate's needs, an unengaged hiring leader who fails to realize the importance of good recruiting, or simply a poorly constructed recruiting process, 99% of the candidates applying to a typical company are likely to walk away with a bad taste in their mouth. And the chances are, your company is typical.

Many organizations focus their sales and marketing messages on being customer-centric but they fail to include their recruiting efforts and candidates in this mix. Recruiting needs to be seen as an extension of the organization's overall brand and held to the same high standards. Recruiting will never make every candidate happy, but treating every applicant with respect, regardless of their suitability, skills, and experience, goes a long way toward protecting the organization's brand.

Why Candidate Experience Matters

Some statistics to consider[4]:

- 83% of candidates say that a negative experience can change their mind about a role or company they once liked.
- 77% of candidates say that their interview experience is extremely important when deciding whether to accept an offer or continue to look at other opportunities.
- 64% of job seekers say that a poor candidate experience would make them less likely to purchase goods or services from that employer in future.

---

[4] Source: CareerArc Employer Branding Study 2017

One of the characteristics shared by every great recruiter, HR manager, and hiring manager I've met is that they can put themselves in the candidate's shoes and see the world—and the company—through their eyes. That's great news for you because, unless your parents own the company you work for, then at some point in your career you were probably a candidate yourself. All you need to do is remember what that was like.

Ultimately, this is good sales: by stepping into the candidate's world, you can engage them (which we will see in Part Two is critical) and, hopefully, entice them to join your organization. So, you have to ensure that each touchpoint they have with the company or with individuals within the company is a positive experience. It starts the first time someone reaches out to them or they see the job posting, and it continues all the way through the offer stage and onboarding (or until they exit from the recruitment process).

That positive experience is critical if you want to keep the best candidates and increasingly, in our social media-fueled world, if you want to attract those candidates in the first place. Often, we recommend our clients undertake a mystery shopper exercise on their recruitment process, so they can understand the candidate's perspective.

Accommodating Candidates

At one stage in my career, I was headhunted by a major IT company. I met with the team in Canada who decided I needed to go to their HQ in the US for the next stage. So, I had to ask my then employer for two days' "vacation," and they flew me down for a grueling two days of interviews.

In total, I ended up attending twelve interviews and meetings, which was exhausting. I got an offer, but I couldn't help wondering what it would be like to work for them if I'd been expected to put my entire life on hold just to get the job. So, when my employer counteroffered, I was only too happy to take the counteroffer and stay put.

The days are far behind us when recruiters and managers could take the view that candidates were lucky to even be considered, and they should be grateful to have an opportunity to work for the company. When candidates have more opportunities and easier access to those opportunities than ever, it's the recruiter that is in competition for the candidates' attention. The market has gone through a complete 180-degree turn, and hiring managers can't expect candidates to put their life on hold and do whatever they can to accommodate the company's requests.

Nowhere does that come through more strongly than when scheduling interviews. You can't automatically expect candidates to attend during working hours. Candidates often don't have the flexibility to meet during core business hours. And if they end up coming back for multiple rounds of interview, there are only so many doctors' and dentists' appointments they can say they are attending before their current employer starts to get suspicious.

> You can't expect candidates to put their life on hold and do whatever they can to accommodate your requests.

Unfortunately, many organizations lack empathy for candidates. Hiring is run in a very one-sided way: "Here are the five interview timeslots we have in the next three days. Hopefully one is good for you, and if not, then this probably isn't going to work out." The subtext is that if the candidate isn't prepared to drop everything—including their current job—for your opportunity, then they're clearly not that interested.

As soon as you see that written down, you realize how unreasonable it is, especially for more senior roles. A VP or SVP typically has their calendar full at least four weeks out, and yet recruiters are calling them and expecting them to come in for an interview the following day.

From an organizational perspective, whether you're a business leader or in HR, you have to adjust your mindset around how and when you interview candidates. Smart organizations understand this. If they've met a candidate once and like them, but multiple managers need to be involved in the interview process, they'll schedule those meetings back to back so the candidate only needs to take an afternoon off, or they'll arrange for the candidate to meet the relevant managers for dinner after hours.

Your Workforce Is Multigenerational, and So Are Your Candidates

Most companies haven't changed the way they hire in twenty years: you could drop a hiring manager from the 1990s into the middle of a present-day interview room, and they'd feel completely at home. All that would have changed is the width of lapels on suits: the questions and the assessment tools would be ones they knew well.

Today, we have more generations active in the workforce than at any time in the past. There are younger generations that grew up with technology and older generations that didn't, and recruitment practices need to reflect that. And yet, few organizations differentiate how they market themselves to different generations, let alone adapting their recruitment processes to them.

For example, some organizations have revamped their recruitment by taking it online and adding gamification features, but older candidates are more likely to be put off—or even scared—by that rather than feeling engaged. Instead of a blanket redesign, you need to consider who your ideal candidates are for a particular role. The audience for a VP role is going to be different from the audience for a junior position, and each will have different expectations.

The Scope of The Candidate Experience

It's easy to assume the candidate experience starts when someone becomes aware of a role, either because they see a job ad or a recruiter contacts them about it. In reality, however, it starts long before that, when the candidate encounters your brand in the marketplace—not as an employer brand but as a consumer brand.

That has other implications for organizations, beyond whether their brand is strong enough to attract top talent. If candidate experience and consumer perception of your brand are so closely linked, it means that you need to consider whether your recruitment processes live up to the expectations created by that brand. For example, if you're a luxury carmaker that consumers see as a white-glove, high-touch brand, your hiring processes must reflect that.

Of course, not every job market is competitive. There's a big difference between hiring in a major city where thousands of organizations are pursuing the same talent, and a provincial town where there may only be a handful of major employers. Even in those smaller locations, however, candidates are highly aware of the reputation of local employers—sometimes more so than their urban counterparts. They can tell you what was happening in those companies five years ago and why you'd want to work for one but not another.

Recruitment Cycles Are Spinning Out of Control

Every major company—and some not so major ones also—has roles that have been open for six months, nine months, or even longer. At The Talent Company, we see this virtually every time we take on a new client in our Recruitment Advisory practice. And when I ask why those roles are still open, the answer is almost always, "We can't find the talent."

Hiring managers, recruiters, and CHROs often complain that roles are taking longer to fill than ever, which is surprising given that technology theoretically gives companies faster and easier access to a wider pool of talent than ever before.

So why are things slowing down? There are two main factors driving the change. First, as I mentioned earlier in the book, most hiring managers don't recruit on a regular basis, so they lack insight and recent experience of the job market and candidates. Second, as I also discussed, recruiters are juggling more and more open positions.

That creates an environment in which inexperienced hiring managers (who often don't recognize that they lack experience) with unrealistic expectations are briefing overworked recruiters who lack the time or the skills to adjust those expectations. Those recruiters then go out into the market, get a few hundred applicants, and pick the ten who are the closest (but not 100%) match for the role. When they present those résumés to the hiring manager—whose expectations remain unchanged and unrealistic—however, the manager rejects them all because they're not a perfect match.

The market has given the hiring manager direct feedback that the requisition is unrealistic. Rather than adjust the brief, however, the hiring manager will tell the recruiter to keep looking, and the cycle repeats, sometimes indefinitely. At that point, one of two things can happen. Either they've been operating well with the position unfilled, in which case they have to question whether they need to fill it at all, or they haven't coped well, in which case the current search strategy isn't serving their needs and they need to change either where they're looking or what they're looking for.

The Candidate Perspective

Long, slow recruitment cycles aren't enjoyable for candidates either. When you apply for a role, attend an interview, get turned down, and then six months later you see that it's still open, it only adds to the disappointment of not getting the job. Recruiters often try to soften the blow of rejection by telling the candidate that they were only rejected because there was someone more qualified. That seemingly innocent lie just makes things worse. However. People apply for a role because they assume (rightly or wrongly) that they are perfect for it, so it's hard for them to come to terms with the fact that the company preferred not to hire anyone rather than hire them.

Alternatively, a recruiter may choose to keep the candidate "warm" in the hope that the hiring manager will relent. So, the candidate applies, gets interviewed, and then they are told they're being considered, but the role is still being advertised weeks later. Is it any surprise, then, that candidates—especially the best and most in-demand—get tired of being strung along and instead withdraw their application voluntarily to pursue opportunities with other organizations?

Too Many Interviews

Another factor that extends the recruitment cycle is the number of interviews a candidate has to attend. In our 2016 *Talent Acquisition Practices* study, we found that candidates typically go through four rounds of interview per role. Talent acquisition leaders are concerned that the number of interviews is increasing, which often happens when hiring managers doubt their own ability to select the right individual for the role. Most hiring managers have made at least one bad hiring decision at some point in their career and had their fingers burned, and those negative experiences often drive them to involve more and more stakeholders in the hiring process.

The increasingly complex nature of business makes it easier to rationalize bringing in those extra people because most roles involve interacting with multiple parts of an organization. So, it's easy for a hiring manager in Marketing to say, "this role involves talking to Finance and Production, so I need them involved in the interview process."

For the time-pressured recruiter, that causes a nightmare. Those additional leaders are all busy and have different schedules. Moreover, the role is outside their area of the business, so they have no reason to prioritize the interview. Before you know it, the process has strung out, and twelve weeks and eight interviews later, the recruiter is sitting down in a room with everybody that interviewed the candidate. Six of them liked him, but two couldn't stand him and say they don't want to work with him. They were asked for their opinion, however, so do you ignore them and hire the candidate anyway, or do you go back to the drawing board?

There's another point to consider alongside the impact on timelines, and that's the impact on the candidate experience. The more people you involve, the more chance there is the candidate may encounter someone they don't like and, if they're part of the interview process, the candidate may assume they're going to be working closely with that person, even if that isn't the case.

What matters most to candidates?[5]

1. *49% - Getting business questions answered*
2. *47% - Receiving timely follow-up to their interview*
3. *46% - Having conversations with company leaders*
4. *41% - Experiencing company culture*
5. *35% - Having a positive experience on site*

It's a no-win situation, so when organizations ask for my advice on sorting out protracted recruiting cycles, the first thing I tell them to do is to identify the critical stakeholders for each role and assess which of those

---

[5] Source: LinkedIn 2016 Global Recruiting Trends Report

people they want involved in the interview process. In most situations, three interviews will be enough: one with the manager, one with a functional/technical specialist, and one to determine organizational fit.

> Rather than calling a candidate back repeatedly, try to build all the meetings into a single afternoon. That may require some hard conversations with stakeholders, and if they can't make time for the interviews when needed then they may not be able to participate in the hiring process.

The Business Impact of Longer Recruitment Cycles

A position that remains open for any length of time is going to have an opportunity cost for the business. If you're lucky, as I said earlier, your unfilled role wasn't business critical and the team manages to keep going. If the role is critical, however, it's likely that other members of the team are backfilling the role on top of their own responsibilities and workload. Or perhaps the team leader themselves steps in. In either scenario, resources get stretched thin and people get frustrated. With organizations already struggling to do more with less, the situation is unlikely to end well. Sixty-hour weeks are nobody's idea of fun, and if you're not careful, there may soon be more roles that need to be filled on that team.

What Is A "Reasonable" Hiring Process?

A reasonable hiring process balances speed to hire and quality of hire. It's not a good idea to rush the process to the point that you can't get the insight on the candidates that you need. At the same time, you don't want a long, drawn-out process where the candidate attends nine interviews (and answers the same questions every time).

You also need to ensure that the candidate isn't rushed into making a decision. Better for them to say it isn't right for them before they take the job than figure it out two or three months later when you've already invested in them.

"It's How We Have Always Done It"

A real challenge in many organizations is that hiring processes are frozen in time—usually sometime in the 1990s or even 1980s. That is, of course, assuming that there is a formal hiring process to freeze: fewer than half of the organizations The Talent Company surveyed for our 2106 *Talent Acquisition Practices* study have documented standard recruitment processes.

In most organizations, hiring tends to be *ad hoc* and evolves with little oversight beyond compliance checks by either HR or Talent Acquisition. As a result, it's impossible to set expectations with a candidate. You can't tell them how to process will go, how many interviews they'll have, who is going to be involved, or even how long the process will take.

It's one thing to tell a candidate at the start that your hiring process is longer than most—that's something candidates should be comfortable with. It's another thing altogether when they've been through what they thought was the interview process and they're expecting a call to say whether or not they got the job, but instead you're asking them to come back for more meetings because more people want to get involved. That kind of thing makes a good candidate question what it would be like working for you—an organization that requires twenty people to make a hiring decision doesn't come across as an entrepreneurial, "get things done" place to work.

That doesn't mean you have to have a single one-size-fits-all process for every position that comes up—that would be impossible. Nor does it mean that hiring processes should be fixed forever once defined. Processes might differ based on the level of the role, the skillset, the department, etc., and they should be constantly evolving to meet the changing demands of the labor market and your business. And every process should be reviewed regularly to evaluate if it is achieving its 3 main goals:

1) **Quality/effectiveness**: Is the organization making effective hiring decisions?
2) **Efficiency**: Are hiring decisions made in a timely manner?
3) **Candidate centric**: Does the process create a positive candidate experience?

Improving the Candidate Experience

Many aspects of the candidate experience are things the recruiter either controls or can influence; others are controlled at a corporate level. There are also many aspects that are beyond the control of either, because—as we saw earlier—they're about public perception. So, let's look at three easy ways to improve the candidate experience based on what you do control.

1. Communication

Candidates consistently complain about communication and authenticity during the recruitment process, which is good news for you because those are both things over which you have full control. It's a matter of looking carefully at how you engage with candidates—a topic we will explore at length in Part Two of this book.

So, improving the candidate experience can start with something as simple as how the organization communicates with them. Are you sending form letters or making personal contact? Are you giving them the full picture or just leading them on while you look for a better candidate?

Yes, your recruiters are under ever-increasing pressure. Yes, your organization gets hundreds of applications every day. Yes, many of those applicants are underqualified. But when it comes to *qualified* candidates, you have to make time to engage them and talk to them, because otherwise the recruitment process is pointless. And you need to find ways to remove underqualified candidates from the process in a way that makes them feel valued, even if the response is fast and automated—for example by inviting them to join the company's talent community (which we discuss in Part Three).

2. Find Out What They Want

As I have pointed out several times in this book, at a given point in time only 14% of candidates are actively seeking a new opportunity, so the first "sale" you have to make is often the idea of changing jobs. Getting A-list candidates interested in a position is critical, but that starts with getting to know them and taking time to understand their current situation and what it would take to make them at least consider a move. It's a process we call "wooing," which we explore more fully in Part Two.

3. Realistic Salary Discussions

Once you get to the stage of wanting to hire a specific candidate, how the offer is made is a major step, which we discuss at length in Part Two. However, one element of the offer above all others has a critical impact on the candidate experience: the salary offer itself. Making a lowball offer to an A-list candidate is an excellent way of ensuring you only ever get to hire B-list candidates.

Many recruiters give too much importance to a candidate's current salary—a very compliance-driven view—rather than thinking like a marketer and trying to find out what it will take to bring the right person into the company. Also, too many recruiters treat the offer phase as a game, opening with a deliberately low offer as a negotiation ploy and waiting to see how or whether the candidate counters. It's an approach that used to work, but in today's highly competitive talent market your first offer may be the only one you get to make. Many candidates are turned off by lowball offers, and they have no qualms about walking away.

The Difference That Makes a Difference

Candidate care can be a powerful differentiator for an organization. It can reinforce your employer brand and show off your organization's culture, which is one of the top three factors in jobseekers' consideration of a job offer.

In Part Two of this book, I set out a new model for managing the recruitment process. It should come as no surprise, given what you've just read, that much of the discussion focuses on the candidate experience.

Reflective Questions

How do candidates feel going through your organization's recruitment and hiring process? Do you solicit feedback from candidates on their recruitment and hiring experiences with your organization? When was the last time you reviewed the recruitment and hiring process for your organization from a candidate's perspective?

How effective is your Talent Acquisition function—and your organization more generally—at communicating with applicants and candidates?

How accommodating is your organization in scheduling interviews with candidates? Are candidates offered interview times outside of core business hours?

How is your recruitment and hiring process perceived by the different generations of candidates your organization recruits?

Do candidates who have previously been declined for an open role re-apply to your organization for future opportunities?

How are rejected candidates informed that they will not be proceeding at different stages of your recruitment and hiring process?

On average, how long does it take for your organization to interview candidates and make a hiring decision? How many stages of interviews do candidates typically go through with your organization?

CHAPTER 7

The Business Impact of Bad Hires

Fixing a broken or subpar recruiting process can only be done by the business as a whole. While talent acquisition is within the scope of HR, a lone HR manager cannot address the problems that create poor hiring decisions on their own. If you want to change behaviors and hiring perspectives it has to carry throughout the business, and hiring managers themselves need to realize the impact and opportunity cost of poor hires.

A poor hiring process impacts the business in many ways, so it never ceases to surprise me that companies don't make hiring more of a business priority. With a poor hiring process, there's a much higher risk of recruiting the wrong person. The direct impact of hiring a low-performing employee is fairly obvious: they're not going to perform the job adequately, they may make expensive mistakes, and they're not going to achieve the outputs and results they were hired for.

The indirect impact is less obvious. A poor performer who stays can have many knock-on effects. First, mistakes or issues with delivery can impact the performance of other members of the team or even other teams. Second, if the poor performer's problems are around attitude or personality, that can cause waves throughout the team and beyond, and impact the performance of everyone around them.

Beyond that, however, there's something else we need to consider, and it's something hardly anyone ever gives thought to: the impact of hiring a "solid" performer, someone who puts their head down and delivers everything demanded of them… and nothing more.

Hiring an OK performer when you could have had a high performer has an opportunity cost too. Imagine hiring a solid performer for your sales team. Their target for the year is $1 Million, and at year end they've achieved it. You may not see that as a problem—after all, they delivered their target. But what if a stellar performer in the same role could have spotted additional opportunities in the market that would have allowed them to close $10 million in the same period? The hiring process that turned off that stellar performer and left you with only that OK performer to hire has just cost you $9 Million. And because they're doing their job and meeting targets, it's going to be hard to get rid of them. So, next year you'll lose out again.

Electronic Recruiting Exchange estimates the financial impact of hiring a top performer at 10 to 100 times the person's compensation[6], so hiring a single top performer at $100,000 per annum salary has the potential to add $1 million to $10 million to a company's revenue every year that they stay with the company.

The Problem with Longer Hiring Cycles

Statistics reveal that the average hiring process has increased significantly in recent years.

- *According to CEB (Corporate Executive Board), since 2010 the average length of the hiring process has increased from 26 days to 68 days (just over 2 months).*

- *60% of job seekers report they have quit an application due to its length or complexity (Recruiting Brief, 2017).*

- *The best candidates are off the market within 10 Days (Source: OfficeVibe, 2017)*

---

[6] Electronic Recruiting Exchange, July 2012

As we saw in Chapter 6, hiring timelines are getting longer. Since 2010, the average time to fill a role has increased by 50% from 42 days to 63 days, despite the urgency many hiring managers feel to fill their position. There are a number of factors that combine to lengthen recruiting cycles.

First, as I pointed out earlier, many leaders do not feel confident in making hiring decisions, so they bring in peers and other stakeholders to do further interviews and get different perspectives.

Second, as I also discussed, it's difficult to get those additional stakeholders to prioritize recruitment activities. When a recruiter sits down with a leader to schedule interviews, they are often discussing timeslots two or three weeks away because in many executives' minds hiring and recruitment simply aren't priorities. We are all busy, and our calendars are full, but it's critical for business leaders to make time for interviews if they are asked.

Third, as we saw, candidates are also busy. They too have full schedules. Recruiters and hiring managers think they can call someone and invite them in for an interview the next day, but often those candidates—especially for more senior roles—won't have an opening in their own calendar for several weeks.

Fourth, when a hiring manager finds a good candidate, there's a temptation to keep looking in case there's a better candidate around the corner. Underpinning that is the assumption that the person you interviewed today will still be available in two months—which ignores the fact that good candidates have other options and opportunities to consider.

Longer cycles make it harder to hire the best candidates. As discussed earlier, a great candidate will probably get multiple offers and they're unlikely to wait to see if you're interested, particularly if it puts at risk the offers they've already received. As a result, even if you were their preferred employer at the start of the process, you can expect those candidates to withdraw their application if you take too long. Another reason why candidates withdraw from a recruitment process that is dragging on, as we saw earlier, is that it raises red flags for them. They'll assume that a slow, painful hiring process is representative of decision making in general in the organization, and that's probably not a work environment they want to commit to.

Either way, if that was your preferred candidate, then you're back to step one with another long slog ahead of you to find the next candidate (who you'll probably put off in exactly the same way). In the meantime, the opportunity costs and operational impacts of having that position vacant accumulate, while other team members get increasingly disengaged from covering the open role.

The best hiring organizations make sure that they go through the interview process quickly. Recruiters and hiring managers alike prioritize recruitment and adjust their schedules accordingly to shorten the recruiting cycle.

When It's OK to Get A Second Opinion

While a poor hiring manager will prolong the hiring process by seeking more and more opinions—and those opinions weigh heavily in their decision—ironically, a good hiring manager also seeks input from others, and that input also weighs heavily in their decision. The difference, however, is down to intent and planning. A good hiring manager decides before the hiring process even begins who is going to be involved and brings them into the process for specific reasons. Typically, those additional interviewers are the hiring manager's own boss and key stakeholders in the role.

Alarm bells should start to ring, however, when you're nearing the end of the scheduled interviews and a hiring manger decides they need someone else to weigh in. Then, after that interview, they remember someone else whose opinion they want to get. Suddenly, a five-step interview process turns into nine steps and no one is any closer to being hired. In those situations, what's usually happening is that the hiring manager asks for more and more input as a way of dispersing responsibility for the hiring decision: if the hire doesn't work out, they can point to all the other people who agreed with them.

The Cost of One "Bad Apple"

If you don't think a single lazy or incompetent employee can damage an entire organization, think again. The negative impact of a poor hire spreads across the organization through their relationships—internal and external—and their interactions with peers. Psychologists say that negative interactions have a far more profound and lasting effect than positive interactions do. Research at several major universities shows that adding just one "bad apple" to a group can drive down performance by 30 to 40 percent, even when other employees are functioning at their peak.[7]

Why? It turns out that a bad apple's destructive behavior is contagious, distracting and dragging down everyone around them. Imagine a team of five built on collaboration. If a new person comes in who isn't living up to their commitments, they're going to take down the whole team—especially if they're a crucial piece of the delivery model.

A recent study on team effectiveness[8] identified three distinct types of disruptive behavior: "deadbeats" who consistently withhold effort; "downers" who persistently express pessimism, anxiety, insecurity and irritation;

---

[7] Wall Street Journal, Oct 24 2011

[8] Source: Felps, Will, Mitchell, Terence and Byington, Eliza. "How, When and Why Bad Apples Spoil the Barrel: Negative Group Members and Dysfunctional Groups". Research in Organizational Behaviour. 2006. Vol. 27, 175–222.

and "jerks" who routinely violate interpersonal norms of respect. A bad apple isn't necessarily someone who behaves in a deliberately disruptive way, however. Over the years, I've worked with many people who were very sociable and loved to talk, but they distracted people from their jobs. Unfortunately, that kind of behavior can easily be overlooked by management because it's not overtly destructive, and eventually it becomes accepted behavior.

The challenge is that you need to act as soon as you start to see disturbing behaviors in the workplace that weren't apparent during recruitment. What typically happens, however, is that the hiring manager makes allowances for the new hire and assumes they merely need more time to adjust. Deep down, they know they've made a mistake and they desperately want the situation to work itself out, but that rarely happens.

Assuming that you do spot the bad apple, what do you do about the situation? Is it a problem that can be resolved through coaching and guidance? Will you sit it out and hope they decide for themselves that they've made a mistake and the role isn't for them? Or are you going to try to performance manage them out as quickly as possible and cover up your hiring mistake, which means you'll need to hire a replacement again?

Grade and Tenure

According to a study by the Society for Human Resources Management[9], the higher an employee's position and the longer they remain in that position, the more it costs to replace them and the harder it is to find suitable candidates. Those two factors together make it tempting to give bad hires in a senior role even more leeway than someone more junior. Interestingly,

---

[9] 2017 Talent Acquisition Benchmarking Report, Society for Human Resources Management

the SHRM study suggests that senior hires are less likely to work out than junior-level hires, but at those higher levels it can take up to two years for the problems to become apparent—if the person doesn't leave first.

Why aren't the problems identified at interview? At those senior levels, candidates are also much less likely to be questioned and challenged about their credentials, especially by a more junior or less experienced interviewer. Often, interviewers are relying on the previous employer to have carried out their own due diligence, especially if the candidate is coming from a major company. On the other hand, if the interviewers are peers then the process is likely to be a series of general meetings with members of the executive team to get their perspective, but the candidate won't be grilled as hard as someone more junior would.

It's Getting Harder to Choose

Despite all the problems a bad hire can cause—and the financial cost of rectifying those mistakes—companies continue to make poor hiring decisions, and it's getting harder to make the right selection decisions. Part of the reason for that, as we saw earlier, is that candidates are better prepared with knowledge about the company and its industry, so they are able to impress an interviewer very quickly. Candidates also have access to far more professional support than ever before: résumé coaches, interview coaches, personal brand coaches, and more. Hiring managers, on the other hand, rarely have coaches on their side to help them.

At the same time, we saw earlier that the pressure to fill open positions quickly, especially in fast-growing organizations, means a hiring manager is more likely to hire a below-average candidate just to fill the role rather than waiting for a better candidate to come along

Ultimately, however, the biggest problem is that recruitment is often re-active: you hire when a position becomes open and has to be filled. The best time to look for candidates, on the other hand, is before that position becomes available—before, in other words, it becomes an emergency. That allows you to take your time finding the best candidates, vet them extensively, and reach the best decision. Unfortunately, that proactive approach only ever happens in about 1% of hiring situations.

Reflective Questions

How effective is your recruitment and hiring process at generating great hires for your organization?

How long is your current recruitment and hiring process?

What is the turnover percentage of new hires within the first year at your organization? Why do new hires leave your organization?

How many poor hiring decisions are made by your organization in a year? What is the cost to your organization of making those poor hiring decisions?

Are senior hires less likely to be successful then more junior hires at your organization?

How confident are your hiring managers in making hiring decisions?

Does your current recruitment and hiring process provide enough insight into whether candidates will be successful in their role with your organization?

PART 2

The Model

In this part of the book, I set out a model for finding and recruiting talent for your organization.

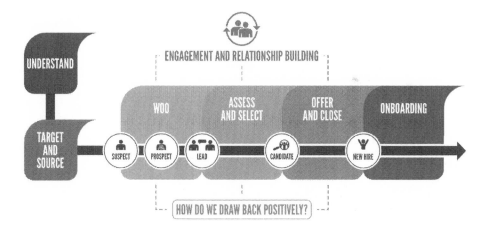

The full model has six phases:

1. **Understand** (Chapter 8) – The recruiter gets clear on the role and the hiring manager's requirements.
2. **Target and Source** (Chapter 9) – The recruiter profiles ideal candidates, researches the market, and creates a target list of potential candidates to approach.

3. **Woo** (Chapter 10) – The recruiter reaches out to potential candidates to get them interested in the opportunity.

4. **Assess and Select** (Chapter 11) – Candidates who are interested go through a series of interviews and assessments that give the hiring manager the data and inputs they need to make an informed decision on whom to hire.

5. **Offer and Close** (Chapter 12) – The hiring manager makes the offer to the chosen candidate, and works to make sure they accept it.

6. **Onboarding** (Chapter 13) – The new hire receives coaching, training, and support to become a productive, performing member of their team and the organization.

Underpinning the model is the need to **build relationships** with candidates and keep them **engaged** throughout the recruitment process (Chapter 14). Without that, we risk losing their interest or, if we get to the offer stage, being turned down.

And finally, at any stage in the process either side can decide to **draw back**, which raises the question, *How do you terminate the <u>process</u> positively, without breaking off the <u>relationship</u>?*

As a candidate moves through the model, it is also helpful to distinguish several distinct changes of status similar to the way sales and marketing teams think of potential customers as they move through a sales cycle. At each step, our questions about the candidate change, as does how we engage them, and analyzing their progress this way gives us deeper understanding and control.

Initially, sourcing identifies a group of individuals in the market whom we believe may be suitable for the role and the company, but who may or may not be interested in it—a group we refer to as **Suspects**. Our primary concern at this stage, therefore, is to determine whether they would even consider a new opportunity.

After the initial contact, if we can confirm that they are potentially interested they become **Prospects**. Our task now is to discuss the opportunity with them so that we can find out if they are interested in the specific role being offered.

Then, if after a follow-up call to discuss the opportunity they are still interested, they become **Leads**. We know they are interested, so before allowing them to progress we need to ascertain that they meet the criteria for the role.

If they do meet the requirements for the position, and assuming that they are still interested at this stage, they are a fully-fledged **Candidate** (with a capital C this time).

Up to this point, the primary contact and decision maker has been the recruiter. Once someone is a Candidate, however, the focus shifts to the hiring manager. Their task—in partnership with the recruiter and all the stakeholders—is to select the individual who ultimately will get the position, the **New Hire**.

CHAPTER 8

Understand

When you know exactly what you're looking for, it becomes much easier to identify the right candidates in the market, build compelling candidate and employee value propositions, and manage expectations internally as well as with candidates.

A major international financial services brand came to us because they wanted to understand their talent market better and build a reliable pipeline of candidates. They were trying to introduce sales coaches into their field sales teams but, because this was a new role for the organization, they had no idea what to look for in terms of job descriptions and experience, or what to pay. So, they asked us to map the market for them.

We identified 225 sales coaches in the geographical areas where they were looking and built a profile of their experience and salary expectations, which we presented to the client. It turns out that a good sales coach is usually someone who started off in sales, progressed to sales manager, and has 10-15 years' experience before becoming a sales coach. Their salary expectations match that experience and what the client was intending to pay was almost half what the market demanded.

Armed with the market mapping results, however, the client's recruiting team was able to build a business case for increasing the budget and strengthening the candidate value proposition so that they would be able to attract the right caliber of candidate. In the end, they hired 18 new coaches who would not even have considered them if they had gone to market with their original salary offer.

Get to Know Your Ideal Candidate

"Understanding"—specifically understanding of the role—is the foundation of the recruiting process. Without it, none of the steps that follow are possible. For each specific role in your portfolio, you need to understand what a great candidate looks like and where they are going to be.

However good your recruiters are, they can't succeed without good candidates. One of the best and easiest ways to find those candidates is to talk to the talent in that functional area within your organization. They'll be able to tell you which events those people attend, which companies are known for the quality of their team in that area, and other good "hunting grounds." That information then needs to go to a dedicated team of sourcers whose job is to go out into the market, find those individuals, and engage them.

And it's not only the recruiters who need that depth of understanding. All the stakeholders in the hiring decision need to be familiar with the specific skills, experience, education, and background that you are looking for, so that you'll be able to target the right candidates effectively. Without that understanding, it's easy to cast a very wide net, which doesn't sound like a problem, but it leads to a lot of wasted time and resources. If you're not targeted in your search, you start recruiting and a month later there's no clear group of candidates and the hiring manager is getting frustrated.

Hiring Internally vs. Externally

As an organization, you need to decide whether your approach to talent is to grow and develop from within or to acquire talent externally, and there's a delicate balance to be struck.

When I was in charge of talent at American Express, the company's focus was very much on developing talent internally. We would hire externally for call center positions with the aim of developing them into roles outside the call center. I had to work hard to challenge that status quo. I couldn't understand why, if we wanted to hire a marketing specialist, we couldn't look for one in the open market rather than hiring somebody from one of our call centers who we thought might have potential but who had no marketing expertise.

Before I joined American Express, about 90% of all open positions were filled with internal talent. In part, that was because it was easier to hire internally and the recruiters didn't necessarily know where or how to source talent externally. My goal was to reduce that to 75%: people still had the opportunity to be promoted and grow internally but at least a quarter of the organization would be coming from the outside, bringing with them a fresh perspective, specialized skills, and the desire to make an impact.

The Intake

Understanding the role begins with a well-constructed brief for the recruiter, but that rarely happens. Hiring managers often view recruitment as just another procurement exercise. At the start of the hiring process, they'll hand the recruiter a job description that lists the responsibilities and compensation. Even when the brief does consider the person rather than the role, it's typically little more than a disordered wish list. To make matters worse, it's often out of date because it probably hasn't been updated since the current post-holder was recruited.

Hiring isn't black and white. There's a lot of grey in it, and organizations that recognize this excel at recruitment. Candidates are unique. They have different experiences and different education. Some candidates will be stronger in some areas, and other candidates in others. If you're lucky, in among the applicants you'll find a few candidates who are a 75% match for the brief or better. So, part of the coaching the recruiter gives the hiring manager should be to understand which points are negotiable. Good recruiters and HR partners sit down with hiring managers and ask detailed questions about the profile they are looking for to fill the job. They help the hiring manager to prioritize requirements and distinguish between "must haves" and "nice to haves."

Even then, the person hired will probably be great at seven or eight out of ten key requirements for a role but terrible at the rest. Meanwhile, someone in a different position, who might excel in those areas, doesn't have them in their role description so they're not putting their strengths to work for the company.

Are You Hiring a Person or Filling a Role?

The best hiring managers look for the best candidates *from an organizational perspective*, find out what their strengths are, and tailor a role to that profile. In that way, they are not just acquiring the best talent for the company, they have that person in a role where they are performing highly at all of the key requirements. At The Talent Company, for example, we don't use job descriptions in our hiring process, for precisely that reason. When I meet a candidate, it's the person I'm interested in. I want to understand where their strengths are, and I'll build a role to leverage those.

Unfortunately, many organizations tie compensation to job descriptions. So, if you add or remove responsibilities, it starts to impact salary and raises compliance issues. And if the role is unionized, or controlled by a professional association, things become even more complicated.

When it comes to the requirements of the role and what constitutes a good candidate, the hiring manager is the expert. They are the person with insight into the skillset they are looking for. Much of that knowledge is inside the hiring manager's head rather than in the brief, however, so before doing any work, the recruiter needs to sit down with the manager for a detailed intake discussion to go through the brief line by line and understand what's behind every aspect.

Part of the task will be to find out from the hiring manager where the best talent is likely to be found. Are they already working for competitors? Are they in other industries? Another factor that feeds into that, however, is awareness of the realities of the market: if the organization is not seen as an A-player, for example, it will be challenging to attract A-list candidates.

They will also need to scan and evaluate internal talent, and whether there is someone already inside the organization who should be considered, how they would need to develop to grow into the role, and whether the investment is justified. Promoting internal talent is always less risky than bringing in outsiders and will significantly increase employee engagement—although at some point every organization needs to bring in fresh talent.

Next, it's about understanding why the position is open, and what has made previous incumbents successful (or unsuccessful) in the role—the traits and behaviors that worked well or didn't work well.

And finally, it can be very powerful to look at past hiring successes. It is useful to reflect on how top performers were recruited, where they came from, and what made them stand out in the interviews—creating what we refer to as a *"How do I hire you again?"* profile.

That discussion can also be expanded to include some of those top performers. In addition to getting a better understanding of who they are, it also creates opportunities for them to refer people in their own network—who may well be very similar to them.

The Recruitment Plan

The brief is about being clear on who you will be recruiting. Equally important is understanding how they will be recruited and creating a hiring plan to achieve that. In the absence of a clear plan, the hiring process is more likely to go off track and get drawn out. Then, as we saw earlier, more and more people get dragged into the process and it becomes difficult to get everybody to schedule time.

That becomes a major dissatisfier for everyone—the recruiter, the candidate, and all the stakeholders—so the sooner you can lock down the process and start blocking out time in people's calendars, the better.

Reflective Questions

Do your recruiters and hiring managers understand current labor market trends?

Are your hiring managers realistic in their hiring needs and ideal candidate profiles? Do they articulate those hiring needs and ideal candidate profile effectively to the recruiters?

Do your recruiters understand the roles for which they are recruiting? Are your recruiters comfortable pushing back if presented with unrealistic hiring expectations?

What proportion of open positions are filled with internal versus external talent? What is the impact on your organization?

Is there a recruitment and hiring plan for every open requisition within your organization?

CHAPTER 9

Target and Source

At any given time, only 14% of people are actively seeking a new position. Once you understand what you're recruiting for, however, you can research where the right talent will be and start to identify all candidates who meet the criteria. Then you search 100% of the market and reach out to candidates who might not have considered you and aren't actively seeking a new role.

One of our clients is a medical marijuana producer based in a small, somewhat isolated rural community. The company had plans to expand dramatically, but their location made it hard to attract the right candidates.

In theory, an ideal hire for them was someone who has grown their own marijuana at home. That made for some interesting screening conversations, but it also created some HR nightmares. There's a big difference between growing marijuana at home and doing it as a 9-to-5 job as an employee of a large company. Also, the industry is very heavily regulated and there's a level of compliance and inspection that didn't sit well with a lot of candidates. As a result, one out of every two people they hired would either leave or be asked to leave in a short space of time because they didn't fit the culture of the organization.

We had to help them redefine what their ideal candidate looked like. It turns out, it's easier to take someone from a heavily regulated, high-security industry like pharmaceuticals and teach them about marijuana than to take a home grower and make them compliant.

Their options were either to attract the right people and get them to relocate, or to move the entire company to somewhere closer to a major city. Getting people to relocate required new messaging. The area where the business is located is a popular spot for vacations—city dwellers refer to it as "cottage country"—so the focus of their value proposition had to be on lifestyle, leaving behind the three-hour commutes of the city, and enjoying the amenities the area had to offer.

Finding Talent

In every industry, to pick the location for an office, factory, or whatever without looking at the supply of talent in the area, and it's too easy for employers to focus on the skills they want without considering whether people will be the right fit for the organization's culture.

Ultimately, the only outcome that matters for recruitment is the quality of the hire. A good hire depends on a strong candidate shortlist, and the better your organization can get at targeting and sourcing, the more candidates you will have in the funnel. That gives you more hiring options which, in turn, usually leads to better quality hires. So, once the recruiter understands who they are looking for, their next task is to find suitable candidates. That breaks down into two separate steps: targeting and sourcing.

Ideally, by the time the hiring manager comes to selecting who to hire, they would be choosing from at least three excellent candidates, any of whom would be a great choice. If your sourcing starts with a small pool, however, you may end up with only one good candidate—if you're lucky—and a number of acceptable but mediocre candidates.

A strong sourcing function gives the organization the capability to provide hiring managers with market intelligence and qualified talent in real time, as the need arises. That level of responsiveness and value helps build trust with internal clients and positions the Recruitment team as responsive, informed, and quality-orientated talent advisors.

Why Sourcing Matters

I am always shocked that Recruitment functions are not more focused on sourcing talent rather than "post and pray." Hoping that the right person will see your job posting and respond is not a sustainable strategy for attracting the right talent. So, you can't afford to leave candidate sourcing to chance; you have to proactively target the right candidates from the outset. However, because organizational leaders don't understand the importance of sourcing or how it differs from general recruitment, they rarely give it the priority it needs, and few organizations have built sourcing functions.

In many respects, an internal sourcing team is like having in-house headhunters. In the pre-computer world it was hard to find candidates, so sourcing was routinely handed off to external headhunters who would do the research and make calls. Now, however, all the information you need to source candidates yourself is available online.

Sourcing itself, can be broken down into three sub-tasks:

1. Generating candidate names
2. Research
3. Cold calling prospects

Few recruiters have time for the standard tasks of recruitment, let alone these additional sourcing tasks, and even when organizations have built an internal sourcing function, it's often just a lone recruiter trying to do all the above.

And yet, many organizations are investing significant amounts of money on third-party search teams to find candidates. When you look at the sums involved, it's easy to make a business case to take a fraction of that money and create a dedicated sourcing team. In the long term, the organization will not only save money, but often will also find that the quality of candidates generated is higher. So, the best organizations are hiring—or developing—sourcers to support their recruiters in much the same way that sales functions split inbound and outbound sales teams rather than trying to have salespeople do both.

Finding Good Sourcers

In sales, a distinction is often drawn between "farmers", "fishers", and "hunters". The same distinction can be made in recruitment. Most recruiters, especially in a "post and pray" environment, are fishers. They set their bait—a well worded job posting—and wait for candidates to come to them. Others are farmers, who invest time in building relationships and strengthening their pipeline. Then, when they need to find the perfect candidate, they have everything they need in place. Very few recruiters are natural hunters.

The Sourcing function can only be as effective as the quality and experience level of the sourcers allow, and you can't just take a traditional recruiter and turn them into a sourcer because the background, skills, and mindset are very different. A recruiter who has only ever worked in a "post and pray" environment—a fisher who is used to having candidates land on their desk who are available and interested—is probably going to struggle if they suddenly have to start cold calling. A good sourcer, on the other hand, is part hunter, part detective. They use all the tricks, tools, and tips of their trade to track down their target individuals and uncover ways to reach them.

Sourcing is, above all, a research task. The best sourcers are rarely to be found inside an existing Recruitment function. Instead, people with the necessary hunter's mindset are more likely to be in outbound sales and marketing teams. That is where you find sales administrators who are used to pulling together target lists for their sales teams—a task very similar to sourcing for recruitment.

These days, most people have an extensive online presence, which makes it much easier to find them. Until someone speaks to them, however, there is no way to know whether they will be a good fit for the role and the company or even whether they will be interested in the position. So, sourcers initially build as big a list as they can initially.

In The Talent Company, our sourcers are typically aiming to identify between a hundred and two hundred possible candidates. Those names then go to someone whose job is to get on the phone and engage them. The big difference between a sourced list of two hundred names and a list of two hundred applicants who replied to an online job posting, however, is that the sourcer is in control of who makes it onto the sourced list and they will only put people on it who they believe are a viable candidate. They may also choose to add a few people who aren't at the right level right now but who could either be a potential source of referrals or someone the sourcer wants to get into the pipeline for future opportunities so that the company can start to build a relationship.

Sourcing Starts with a Plan

Whether you are building a new sourcing team from scratch or strengthening an existing sourcing team, having the right people in place is just part of the solution. The other critical element is sound workforce planning.

You can only build a proactive sourcing model when you understand what the key roles are that your organization needs to focus on for the next six to twelve months, and in Chapter 15 we will look at how to create a workforce plan for your organization. The workforce plan translates the business's strategic goals into talent impacts: what skills need to be in place, in what numbers, when? HR can then look at what resources are available internally, what can be developed from within, and what will have to be acquired externally. That workforce plan thus becomes a mandate for the sourcing function.

A proactive plan-driven sourcing model allows you to build pipelines before you need them. Then, when a position becomes available, you can start with a list of candidates who have already indicated that they would be interested and feed candidates directly into the interview process, which cuts sourcing time down dramatically. Searching before the pressure is on also allows sourcers to target specific skillsets more accurately, identify higher quality candidates, and reach people who would probably not have responded to a 'post and pray' recruitment ad.

Additional Roles in Sourcing

The best sourcer in the world will struggle to fill a position on their own. They are just one part of a multifunctional team built around two simple principles: collaboration and leveraging people's individual strengths. When we work with an organization that has an existing Recruitment team, we'll take time to sit with each recruiter and find out how they operate. Ultimately, the final size and structure of the team will depend on the size of the organization, the budget available (and the appetite for further investment), and the kind of roles that are being recruited.

What makes a good sourcer?

The following are common traits and characteristics of successful senior sourcers:

- *Experts at identifying quality candidates and spotting business and market trends early.*

- *Comfortable with a variety of sourcing channels including social media.*

- *Interested in discovering new and emerging candidate sourcing methods.*

- *Out-of-the-box thinking when it comes to engaging candidates.*

- *Professional phone demeanor*

- *Able to apply critical thinking and decision making when interacting with candidates.*

- *Organized and methodical in their use of CRM, LinkedIn or other tools.*

- *Pride in their personal brand and relationships.*

- *Experienced with talent identification, cold calling and networking for candidates.*

- *Confident (generally extroverted), self-disciplined, and often have past experience in a sales role.*

- *Passion for building and nurturing relationships with candidates, and a genuine interest in speaking with people.*

Different people have different comfort levels in the various aspects of search, and very few recruiters are strong in all areas. There are recruiters who like to be out talking to people—they are often also the ones who hate the admin side of recruitment, so we'll suggest having an administrator to take care of all the paperwork. Other recruiters are great at generating names, but they may not like talking to candidates or engaging them. So, we may suggest creating a role that is responsible for the initial conversation with candidates, and as they become interested in the position they are passed on to someone else in the team who is great at candidate assessment. You also need account managers who are responsible for updating business leaders regularly and driving the search work for the team. Finally, some organizations have recruiters who specialize purely in the candidate experience—their job is to keep candidates warm, informed and in a positive frame of mind. In many respects, they act as account managers for the candidates.

Talent Mapping

One of our clients is the head of HR for a large consumer packaged goods company. They were looking for a new CMO and asked us to identify suitable candidates and make the initial approach. The market map we created listed not just CMOs but also all VPs of marketing and above at other companies in their industry in the same region. We then tracked down contact data for each person on the list and created individualized plans for approaching each person, setting out how we would contact them and what the candidate value proposition would be for each individual.

Talent mapping—identifying where in the market candidates are likely to be, as we discussed in Chapter 2—is one of the first steps in sourcing. Just as sales teams rely on Customer Relationship Management software to manage their pipeline, recruiters have *Candidate* Relationship Management (CRM) tools at their disposal as we saw in Chapter 4.

CRM allows sourcers to map talent to multiple opportunities. With it, the sourcer can quickly and easily identify and follow contacts by specific category, even if they don't have a résumé to search against, organize them into pipelines, and track and report metrics for those pipelines. The choice of CRM tool is critical to the effectiveness of a sourcing practice. Sourcers not only utilize the CRM's capabilities to pipeline, manage and nurture their candidates but also to track and report the impact of the sourcing function on recruitment and on the broader organization.

Sourcing with LinkedIn and Other Platforms

Technology can be a major tool in making sourcing timely and proactive. It can also make the recruiter's life simpler, but only if they have the time and ability to properly utilize the tools available to them. Even something as commonplace as LinkedIn can be valuable when used correctly, and it's one that surprisingly few recruiters know how to use properly. For example, sourcing can start with something as simple as typing the job title and location into LinkedIn: in a matter of seconds, the platform will generate a list of hundreds of potential candidates which you can then refine. Even searching on Google can yield a list of candidates—and the more senior a candidate is, the easier they can be to find online.

The search can also empower sourcers to push back against unrealistic briefs. When we coach sourcers for our clients, one of the points I make sure we bring up is that if a search for a specified skillset returns only a dozen names, the criteria are probably too narrow, and the search needs to be expanded.

Of course, you can't judge a candidate from their profile alone; you need to speak to them. Many great candidates have a weak résumé, while many weak candidates have professional résumé writers who make them look great on paper. So, if you're starting with a small list, you may find after those conversations that there are no suitable candidates at all and you have to start again.

As we saw in Chapter 4, most organizations have a huge number of contacts in their database that they never look at once the role they applied for has been filled. Platforms like LinkedIn, ZoomInfo, and Hoovers, combined with the information in an existing ATS or CRM, make it possible for organizations to source from a large targeted pool of talent and identify potential candidates with the exact skills, experience, previous job titles, and seniority they are looking for.

And different platforms can be better for different briefs. For example, for blue-collar roles LinkedIn searches may yield few prospects. A few years ago, we were hired to map the home inspectors market. There are not many home inspectors on LinkedIn. However most of them are independent business owners and want to be found, so Google yielded hundreds of their websites along with the regional industry associations they belong to.

Technology can be an incredibly powerful tool in recruitment, but only if you have the right people hunting for talent and you give them time to use the technology. I've been into organizations that are spending $500,000 every year buying recruitment platform licenses for every recruiter because they've been told by a salesperson that it will solve all their talent sourcing problems. When they realize that those problems haven't gone away, they hire us to figure out what's gone wrong.

Inevitably, HR leaders are pointing fingers at the recruiters, saying it's their fault for not using the technology properly. However, when you look at how recruiters are spending their time, they're too busy and overwhelmed to use the platforms to research and hunt for candidates. All they have time for is posting job listings, so they're using it as just another—albeit massive—job portal.

Growing the List

Once the initial list has been generated, there are many ways to add more names. That way, even if you're starting with a small seed list, it can quickly become much longer.

1. The sourcer needs to sit down with the hiring manager to expand, synthesize, and polish the list: are there any candidates they already know—personally or by reputation—and are there any that the recruiter shouldn't contact?
2. People with similar backgrounds and experience usually know each other. so the list can be grown further by talking to existing employees in similar roles who may be hooked into relevant networks, whether through professional communities or previous employers.
3. New hires are another good source of leads. If the sourcer has identified candidates who work for their previous employer, it can be useful to get their feedback on those individuals and also ask if anyone is missing from the list who should be on it.

4. Another way of expanding the list is to include people who are more senior than the role requires, but who may be able to refer other people from their network.

Once the list has reached 100-200 names, the sourcer can start to look for contact info for each potential candidate using company websites, social media, and sales tools like Zoominfo and Hoovers. Armed with a way to contact each candidate, the sourcer can then develop a personalized strategy for approaching them individually.

Using Third Party Sourcing

Even if you're building a sourcing capability in-house, it doesn't necessarily need to handle every aspect: some areas can still be outsourced. For example, we have clients who task us with researching the market and create a candidate list for their internal sourcing team to make the initial approach. For example, they may bring us a request like "We are going to be creating a new field engineering team. Can you research a list of all the field engineers working locally?" We prepare a list of 400-500 field engineers in the region, and their sourcing team takes over from there.

Of course, even when we're doing the initial stages of sourcing, the client's input is priceless. When we were helping the CPG company I mentioned above to find a CMO, we mapped the market and found 275 potential candidates who fit the profile they were looking for. Then we sat down with the client and went through the list one-by-one. Combining our research with their intimate insider knowledge of the industry, we were able to reduce that list down to 120 candidates that we then approached to assess their level of interest and start engaging them.

The client ended up interviewing 10 candidates and made a hire. The CHRO estimated that the process saved them at least $60,000 compared to using a traditional executive search firm.

Integrating Sourcing into an Existing Recruitment Function

There are three broad models an organization can use to integrate a specialized sourcing discipline into their Recruitment function.

1. The pod sourcing model
2. The centralized sourcing model
3. The outsourced sourcing model

Which one an organization chooses will depend on how the Recruitment function is currently structured and where they want to take it.

The Pod Sourcing Model

In this model—also known as the decentralized sourcing model—sourcers, recruiters, and administrators come together in multidisciplinary teams to fill open positions. Typically, each pod supports a specific business unit. The recruiter is the pod leader and the primary point of contact between the pod and its business unit, acting as both account manager and business partner. The sourcer's role, meanwhile, is to find qualified candidates for open positions within the business units the pod supports, and the administrator provides support to the pod.

Pros

The pod model ensures that the sourcer and the recruiter are on the same page. Usually, the recruiter has the initial intake discussion with the hiring manager, and the next person they talk to is the sourcer to explain what's needed.

Because pod members share a common goal of delivering specific recruitment services to their clients, the pod model increases ownership, control, and accountability for recruitment within the team.

This way of working also allows pod members to build a deeper understanding of the specific requirements of the business unit they support, and develop closer relationships with that business unit more quickly.

Cons

Of course, it's not all good news. The Pod model makes it harder to take advantage of economies of scale. There's a lot of duplication of roles, and staffing multiple pods effectively often requires organizations to significantly increase headcount and investment in their overall Recruitment team. At the same time, the pod model discourages the sharing of work between pods, so it's not unusual for one pod to be underutilized while another is overworked.

The pod model also encourages the development of siloes that further reduce the scope for creating synergies and economies of scale. With teams working independently on their requisitions, there is little incentive or opportunity for broad competitive and market intelligence gathering and reporting that could benefit the organization as a whole.

In the same way, pods are unlikely to pool their candidates. You may have five different teams all recruiting for similar roles—marketers, for example—but systems are seldom set up to ensure that candidates can be shared between pods (and, therefore, between business units). Candidates, however, don't understand the internal organization, so once they are dealing with one team, they are unlikely to initiate contact with others in the same company.

Siloes become further entrenched because pods often have a view that their business is different from the others. Teams develop their own processes and practices and are often unwilling to learn from and adopt systems developed in other pods.

Finally, in the pod model, sourcers usually have neither the opportunity nor the remit to build pipelines in advance of roles becoming open. So they only work on open positions and it's hard to source proactively.

The Centralized Sourcing Model

In the centralized sourcing model, recruiters, sourcers, and administrators work in teams based on their role: all the sourcers in one team, the administrators in another, and the recruiters in a third. These teams them align with the business in whichever way best matches their own needs and way of working. Typically, that means the recruiters align with business units to match the alignment of HR in general—particularly where business units have an assigned HR business partner—while the sourcers align themselves by skillsets or functional specialties (one sourcer building a pipeline for sales candidates, another for marketing, another for technology, etc.).

Pros

Building teams around recruitment functions makes collaboration and the sharing of knowledge, candidates, and best practices easier, and—because the focus of each team is centralized—processes, SLAs, and standards are usually applied more consistently than in the pod model.

If your organization is trying to build proactive pipelines of external talent, the centralized sourcing model is the most effective model and the easiest to manage. It avoids many of the siloes created by the pod model and creates economies of scale. At the same time, sourcers can be reassigned quickly to meet changes in demand and the model is easily scalable without requiring a significant increase in recruiting headcount or budget.

Cons

The challenges with this model derive from the disconnect it introduces between sourcers and recruiters. Arranging staff by function can create an "us vs. them" culture within the Recruitment function where it feels like the sourcers find the candidates and the recruiters "take" them away from them, so sourcers never feel the thrill of knowing that "their" candidate got the job.

Detaching sourcers from business units and their assigned recruiters makes it harder for sourcers to foster close partnerships with the recruiters—and the business units—they support. It also diminishes the depth of industry- and line-of-business-specific knowledge that sourcers are able to accumulate.

It can also create control and ownership issues around Recruitment resources between business units. Because HR is usually structured around lines of business, the larger, more influential business units often end up calling the shots and monopolizing the time of the strongest sourcers.

The Outsourced Sourcing Model

Few organizations have the luxury of adding headcount and resources to their Recruitment function on a full-time basis. The outsourcing model allows them to leverage third-party firms to act as a sourcing arm, build the candidate pipelines they need, and give in-house recruiters better candidates to work with.

When an organization only needs to strengthen its sourcing function for a short period of time or to meet a specific need, it can be tempting to hire freelance sourcers on a contract basis or use offshore sourcers. The problem with both of those options is that neither is likely to have in-depth expertise in the organization's market. It's one thing to pull together a list of the top marketing people in the market. It's another thing to know which companies have the best talent working for them, how your employer brand compares to them, and the latest market trends in pay and benefits. Using offshore sourcers can also introduce additional language and cultural barriers that reduce the effectiveness of your pitch.

It's in these situation that organizations like The Talent Company can have the greatest impact.

Pros

The outsourced sourcing model can be the easiest to implement (and to shut down once the need for it has passed) and has no headcount impact. It is also flexible and scalable.

Cons

The biggest challenge with this approach is finding sourcers of the right caliber. Sourcing is a relatively new discipline within recruitment and experienced practitioners are rare outside major cities.

Another major challenge is that when you hire an external party, you lose control of the message, and the branding. At the same time, many organizations have concerns about quality—although these can be mitigated by putting in place strong SLAs and processes.

From a capability-building viewpoint, however, the biggest downside is that in the long term, any data and market intelligence the sourcers gather tends to stay with the outsourcers rather than coming into the organization, prolonging the organization's dependence on external sourcers.

The Power of Outsourcing

Major organizations with large, well-funded Recruitment functions often have the flexibility already to deal with fluctuating demand for sourcing. The greatest challenges are faced by mid-sized organizations that can't afford to build their capability quickly. For those organizations, it can seem as though the only option is to hire an external search firm and incur full search fees. But then, if you find two candidates who fit the organization and you hire them both, the fees are doubled.

In that situation, the outsourced sourcing model can be a valuable alternative. When clients outsource to The Talent Company it's on a project basis, and the fees can be 50%-67% lower than a typical search fee. And, because it's a project fee, it stays the same whether you hire one candidate or ten.

Need Reliable Outsourced Support?

The Talent Company provides Talent Mapping and Talent Pipelining services for organizations across North America. For more information, click here:

www.thetalent.co/TalentPipelining

Reflective Questions

Are your recruiters "farmers," "fishers," or "hunters"?

Does your organization recruit only job seekers who are active in the market?

Does your Talent Acquisition function research and target talent or rely on posting positions to attract talent to apply to your organization?

Are your recruiters equipped with the proper tools and platforms to re-search potential candidates for your organization?

Are your recruiters comfortable cold calling candidates and selling them on your opportunities?

Could your organization benefit from outsourcing candidate research and sourcing to a third-party firm?

CHAPTER 10

Woo

Would you rather sort through thirty qualified candidates or a thousand random people who responded to an ad? Once you've researched the market and built your target list, your next step is to approach your top targets and get them interested enough to consider you. You'll need to tailor your value proposition and pitch, and keep them interested if they bite. If you can approach a hundred targets and interest thirty of them, you have thirty qualified individuals to consider rather than the one or two possible who might have replied to an open posting.

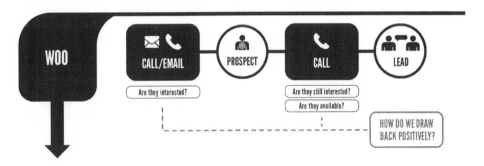

The Woo step is about getting candidates interested in the opportunity. Sales professionals know the importance of getting to know their potential buyers. In the same way, a recruiter needs to get to know their candidates, especially as they get further into the recruiting process. That starts with their understanding of the position, the organization, and the market: building on their initial intake meeting with the hiring manager, the recruiter reflects on what makes this an excellent opportunity for the candidate.

The Candidate Value Proposition

The first stage of wooing a target candidate is to formulate what I call a "candidate value proposition" to appeal to them individually. If you want to hire the best candidates, you can't afford to send a standard offer letter and wait for the response. You need to understand what matters to each candidate, so that when you get to the point of making an offer you know how to sell the opportunity to them. For example, if money is important, you know that you need to focus on salary and benefits; if career path and development are more important, then that's what you focus on. Smart recruiters coach interviewers in advance so that they can work on each candidate's hot buttons, and that becomes even more critical once you're ready to make an offer.

Recruiters often talk about an employee value proposition. However, I created the concept of a candidate value proposition for two key reasons. First, because the employee value proposition is too inward-focused: its purpose is to remind current employees why they love working there, and that doesn't always translate well externally. Second, because the employee value proposition is too generic: the candidate value proposition is tailored to a specific candidate.

The candidate value proposition sets out why your organization is a great place to work—not just in general, but specifically for this candidate—and why the role they are being offered is the right opportunity for them at this moment in time. That might include their future career path, the impact of the role, development opportunities, who they will be working with, and the type of work they will be involved in.

To create a candidate value proposition, you start with the general employee value proposition: why employees join your organization, why they stay, and what makes it a great place to work. However, you then rewrite that employee value proposition from the individual candidate's perspective. In making that translation, some things will stay the same; others you will need to tailor to the individual, using what you've found out about them not only from your research but from talking to them. Notice, however, that I'm not suggesting that you create personalized offers for every candidate—just that you emphasize different aspects of the offer for different candidates.

First Contact: The Elevator Pitch

It's useful to remember that if you're calling a candidate, other organizations are probably calling them too. And the better the candidate, the more calls they are getting, so you need to differentiate yourself: you have to find something that will make your message stand out and make the candidate want to call you back.

At one stage in my career, I was getting 20 to 25 calls from recruitment firms every week. All of them would leave messages, but out of all the calls I received, only one or two stood out enough for me to call them back. They were personal messages that didn't sound scripted. They were authentic, welcoming, and upbeat.

Interestingly, if you're an internal recruiter from the hiring organization, that is often enough to set you apart from other calls the candidate is getting. Very few corporate recruiters make calls themselves, so candidates are used to getting calls from agencies and headhunters. As a result, however, there's something very special about getting a call from a company itself that starts, "Hi. This is Simon Parkin from American Express...."

Many recruiters make the same kind of mistake that novice salespeople make, which is to try to close the deal on the first call. Candidates are easily put off by a long and detailed approach, so you can't make the first call or email long enough to cover the candidate value proposition, to gauge interest, and to assess whether they are a good potential fit for the role.

Before you engage a new candidate, therefore, you need to turn the value proposition into a succinct elevator pitch that will get their attention. The idea is not to lay everything out immediately: the objective of the initial contact is only to get the candidate interested enough that they will agree to a follow-up call where you can tell them more about the opportunity.

Finally, a critical element of that first contact that many recruiters forget is the call to action: what you want the candidate to do next. The more control you can maintain over the process, the better, and if you tell people how to respond they are far more likely to do so than if you leave things open and hope they will call you back.

The Discovery Process

Finding out a candidate's priorities, requirements, and expectations isn't hard. Most of the time, all you need to do is ask.

- What do you enjoy about your current role?
- What don't you enjoy?
- What do you feel is missing?
- Why are you looking to move now?

That should lead to an open and authentic conversation. For example, if someone has just told you that their current work environment is too chaotic and entrepreneurial and they're looking for a slower, steadier pace, then you need to compare that to your company. If your organization is equally fast-paced and entrepreneurial, you know they won't be a good fit. The earlier you can get those kinds of conversation out in the open, rather than going through the process for its own sake with someone who ultimately is going to say no, the happier everyone will be.

Many recruiters shy away from asking the hard questions, but even in the first phone call, you can ask "What are your salary expectations?" As the process advances, you can check in periodically and see if their position has changed: "Last time we spoke, you said you were looking for around $80,000. Now you know a little more about our organization, is that still the number you're thinking of?" That's a conversation that you couldn't have had with most candidates just a few years ago. However, the world has moved on, and more people are willing to open up early on.

When you ask those questions, it shifts the initial discussion. Rather than just talking through the opportunity, you can find out about the candidate, their situation, their aspirations, and their requirements. And the conversation is the same, whether you're a recruiter reaching out cold to someone you've identified as a good prospect, or the candidate has approached you.

The Follow-Up Call

The opportunity description is a core part of the follow-up call. This is your first opportunity to sell the candidate on the role itself, which is why getting the opportunity description right is so important.

Another important aspect of this call is setting expectations around who will be involved in the recruitment process, how long it will take, the steps the candidate will have to go through, any background checks required, how you will communicate the results of each step, etc.

Opportunity Descriptions

Too many recruiters send a job description and a covering email rather than taking the time to understand what will resonate with a candidate. The problem is, job descriptions aren't designed to sell the role: they simply list the requirements and responsibilities. So, the next task is to take the job description and the candidate value proposition and turn them into an opportunity description.

Marketers draw a distinction between "features" (the physical characteristics of their product or service) and "benefits" (the payoff to the buyer of choosing it rather than a competitor's offer). Recruiters need to learn to think the same way. Where the job description focuses on features of the job (hours, location, responsibilities, the benefits package, etc.), the opportunity description should focus instead on the benefits *for the candidate* of taking the job.

Notice, by the way, that we're not using "benefits" in the HR sense of the term (medical insurance, leave entitlement, travel cards, etc.). Pay and benefits are a major factor for most candidates, but many candidates put other aspects of the offer ahead of those, and different people will respond to different motivations, many of which aren't captured by standard job descriptions. For example, some candidates will think ahead to their career path and prospects, and the organization's employer brand may into play. Others may be more excited about how the organization contributes to the community or its environmental practices. A Java developer is likely to be more excited about a role that offers cutting-edge development opportunities than in a role maintaining old systems.

Reflective Questions

How effective are your recruiters and hiring managers in selling candidates on joining your organization?

How authentic and realistic is the messaging provided to candidates within your recruitment and hiring process?

Is your candidate messaging customized to reflect what matters most to each individual candidate?

Why do employees join your organization, why do they stay, and what makes your organization a great place to work?

What makes your organization different? Why should candidates to consider working for you?

Do your recruiters have open and authentic conversations with candidates?

How effective are your job postings in attracting attention and engaging candidates?

CHAPTER 11

Assess and Select

A pipeline is only as good as the talent you get from it. A machine can't do that for you: candidates need to talk to real people. Technology and assessments can support the process and provide additional insight, but you can't base a hiring decision on that alone. You still need a trained and engaged hiring manager to assess whether a candidate has the right fit, the right potential, and the right profile.

In the Woo phase, we took the list of Suspects generated, narrowed it down to Prospects who were interested in considering a new opportunity, and then further, to Leads who are interested in the specific role being offered to them. In the Assess and Select phase, we identify qualified Candidates and select the individual (or, potentially, individuals) who will receive an offer. Ultimately, only a trained and engaged hiring manager can make that assessment of whether a candidate has the potential, the right profile, and fit.

Organizations spend hundreds of thousands of dollars on sourcing campaigns to portray themselves as a top employer and to develop stronger talent sourcing channels. But recruitment is not just about sourcing talent. It's about finding the right candidate for the organization. That's why assessment is the most critical stage of this model. If you can't assess great talent, you shouldn't be a recruiter. Without that skill, you'll struggle because even though your sourcing activities deliver good candidates, you can't be sure that you'll select the right ones.

At the same time, while someone may be a good candidate for the role, it doesn't follow that they are a good candidate for your organization. Top talent at one organization may not be top talent at another. So, the assessment phase addresses multiple questions:

- Can this person do the job?
- Will this person be a great fit for the organization?
- Will this person be a great fit for the team?
- Will this person have a future with our company?

The criteria for that decision will come from the intake conversation the recruiter has with the hiring manager, and the decision itself is made following a series of interviews and debriefs. Those interviews and debriefs are the heart of this phase.

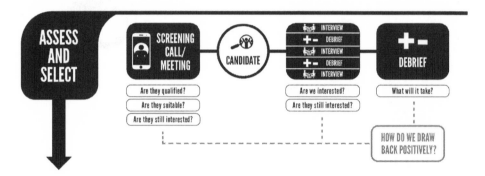

Of course, no single candidate will be a perfect match for a role. So, at any moment in time, there could (and should) be multiple candidates under consideration. We aren't dealing with commodities: every candidate will have drawbacks and advantages, and the assessor's task is to figure out who is most likely to succeed in the role and in the organization.

That task becomes harder because the interviews are usually going to be with different stakeholders, each with their own opinion and assessment, and it's unusual for them all to agree on the same individual. And the more people you involve in the process, the harder it is to make a decision. Often, the recruiter ends up facilitating a selection discussion but the hiring manager should be the ultimate decision maker, taking into account various people's opinions (and overriding them as required).

Creating A Robust Assessment Process

The assessment and selection process needs to be robust enough to give the hiring manager the insight they need to make a decision. The deeper the insight you have into what makes a candidate tick, the better your hiring decisions will be, and a superficial assessment and selection process inevitably leads to poor hiring decisions.

The key lies in identifying and understanding the attributes, behaviors and competencies that are critical for the hire (during the Understand phase) and using these to drive the Assess and Select phase. If, at the end of the process, they still wish they had more information then the process is not fit for purpose.

In terms of poor process, it usually happens for one of two reasons.

1. The process is not robust enough. Interviewers spend an hour with a candidate, part of which is eaten up by small talk, and another part walking through the résumé, and there just isn't time to get to know the individual.
2. The process is too robust. There are too many people involved, and the process takes too long.

An effective process strikes a balance between those two extremes. Exactly where that balance should be will depend on the organization and its capabilities.

The Dangers of Assessment Tools

As we saw in Chapter 4, many organizations use automated tools in their assessment process. While these are useful, they can be expensive. And there is also a risk that goes along with automation: It's tempting for a hesitant hiring manager to abdicate responsibility for their choice, and assessment tools make that easy.

Unfortunately, assessment vendors are only too happy to play along and tell hiring managers what they want to hear: that they'll be able to put their list of a hundred candidates into the tool and it will pick the top five. In reality, however, assessment tools provide valuable insight, but they are decision-*support* tools, not decision-*making* tools. Assessment results must be validated by hiring managers interacting with candidates personally. Ultimately, the choice has to be theirs not the computer's. With that in mind, the best way to use assessment tools is to get better insight into a candidate and to suggest areas that need to be probed more deeply in interview.

A Weak Link in Recruiting

When I was writing this book, I had a meeting with the HR leader at a large software company. They had invested heavily in software tools to support recruitment, and they had exemplary processes and the resources to implement those processes. And yet, they were struggling to hire the right people. Why? Because their hiring managers didn't know how to make a decision. Unfortunately, there's often a direct correlation between how much an organization has spent on assessment tools and how much the hiring managers lean on those tools to make the hiring decision for them.

When an organization has a strong assessment and selection process in place, it always chooses the best candidates available to it. Sadly, assessment and selection processes in most organizations aren't that effective and companies are struggling to identify good talent when it walks through their door.

The best recruiting practices tend to be found in large professional service firms: management consultancies, law firms, systems integrators, etc. The differentiator is that these are organizations that invest in assessment and selection training for everyone actively involved in recruitment. The way to catch up with those leading organizations is to train hiring managers to make the decision rather than rely on technology to make it for them. In that, recruiters also have a role to play as coaches and advisors.

The Best Assessment is an Interview

As I said above, interviews need to be supported by a range of assessment tools to give the hiring manager the insights and data they need to make the hiring decision easier and clearer. At the same time, there's a balance to be struck between getting all the data you need, and not overwhelming the candidate or otherwise creating a negative experience.

Part of being a great interviewer is the ability to get the information you need out of candidates so you can decide whether they should go forward. Sadly, too many interviewers are content to work through a list of questions, checking them off as they go, and relying on the gut feeling they got in the first few minutes of the interview. That initial feeling is inevitably based on personal bias and formed without any meaningful input from the candidate about their behaviors and competencies. And, as we saw in the discussion on hiring clones in Chapter 3, it can lead to some terrible hiring decisions.

Liar, Liar, Résumé on Fire!

Despite high profile scandals and investigations into fake credentials and diploma mills, candidates continue to lie on their résumés. One study a few years ago found that one in four new hires admits to providing organizations with less-than-accurate information during the hiring process. More recent research suggests that number may now be closer to 86%. Whatever the exact proportion, the fact remains that many candidates are padding their experience, education, responsibilities, and accountabilities. On the other side of the desk, recruiters and hiring managers lack the skills and experience to validate what they are saying and cut through the fiction to properly assess their application.

It would be tempting to assume that lying in an application is harder in the age of LinkedIn. But, LinkedIn profiles aren't validated. Often, employees will leave an organization and "forget" to update their profile. Later, if they inflate the grades and titles, former work colleagues are unlikely to question it, if they even notice. And reference checking isn't much help because data privacy laws in most countries prevent organizations from confirming much beyond the fact that someone was employed between two dates. What, then, is the answer?

Good Behavioral Interviewing

One of the most powerful techniques to use alongside assessment tools is behavioral interviewing. Behavioral interviewing carried out by a trained interviewer is the most reliable and valuable assessment. Unfortunately, most interviewers confuse behavioral interviewing with asking *behavior-based* interview questions, which is not the same thing.

Many interviewers, however, ask candidates to talk about a situation and take whatever response the candidate gives without probing. Let's say a hiring manager is looking for someone to work in a high-pressure environment with tight deadlines. They might ask "Tell me about a time when you worked on a project where there was a tight deadline and lots of pressure." That's a great opening question, but 90% of interviewers will listen to the answer, scribble down some notes, and move on to the next question in the interview guide. A smart interviewer will start probing and understanding: "How did that make you feel? How did you respond?" Then they might discover that the candidate made it through the single project they talked about, but they had to go on sick leave for three months to recover.

Worse still are situational interview questions that ask what the candidate would do in a hypothetical situation. While the answer may give you some insight into how the interviewee thinks, it tells you nothing about their experience or how they would react in real situations in the heat of the moment.

The key to good behavioral interviewing is to not take a candidate's first answer at face value. Skilled interviewers probe the candidate to uncover and validate the behaviors the candidate would need to be successful in the role. At Accenture, talent acquisition is an organizational priority. When I worked there, any manager who wanted to get involved in the interview process had to attend an obligatory three-day course on behavioral interviewing. They were trained to ask just three questions in a 90-minute interview and spend half an hour on each. We wanted interviewers to probe and validate every answer. That's how you can truly assess whether someone really has done what they're saying, and they could do it again if needed.

Good behavioral interviewing is a conversation. The aim is to get candidates to come up with the best examples they can, because that will give the interviewer the best insight into whether they are a good fit and the best opportunities for probing. The behavioral interviewer's aim is to ensure not only that what the interviewee did was good but also that it wasn't pure chance; that the inteviewee understands how they made the decision to act the way they did; that they are aware of their feelings and reactions to what was happening; and that they can explain their decisions.

The more comfortable you can make the candidate during the interview, the better their responses will be. Some organizations even go as far as to give candidates their behavioral interview questions in advance so that they can prepare. Since a well-trained behavioral interviewer can quickly see through a "manufactured" answer, the benefits of having candidates bring their best answer far outweigh any risk arising from giving them the questions ahead of time.

Competency vs. Behavior

A critical distinction in behavioral interviewing is between competencies and behaviors. The core objective of good behavioral interviewing is to understand how an individual acts or reacts in particular situations and what drives their behaviors. It goes beyond experience and draws out the factors that will make them either a great hire or merely a good hire. For that knowledge to have value, however, the interviewer needs to be clear on the specific behaviors and competencies they are looking for in a candidate, and which of those are critical to success in the role.

It's also useful to triangulate by having candidates interviewed by two interviewers who are have both been trained in behavioral interviewing. The interviewers shouldn't ask the same questions, however: they should each be looking for different attributes of the candidate and building up a richer, more complete picture between them.

Assessing Fit

Evaluating a candidate's education, experience, and skills is the easy part of hiring. The more challenging part is determining their fit, but it is a critical aspect of the Assessment stage.

Interviewers need to start by understanding the organization's values and culture as well as the desired characteristics, behaviors, and competencies required for the job. Too often, a I said earlier, interviewers don't look beyond a candidate's first answers, and they end up judging the candidate based on their appearance and likeability and whether they "clicked" with the candidate (with the risk, as we saw in Part One, of hiring a "clone").

A skilled interviewer can gain insights into a candidate's values, past behaviors, drivers, and competencies, and behavioral interviewing is the best way to get those insights. The problem is that most organizations—and interviewers—pay lip service to behavioral interviewing.

On the final day of Accenture's behavioral interviewing course, we would bring in MBA students for the managers to interview, and professional assessors. It wasn't enough to just attend the course—you had to pass, however senior you were. I remember one partner being told they would have to retake the course six months later to, and in the meantime *they were not allowed to interview or interact with any candidates.*

Could your hiring managers be better at assessing candidate fit?
The Talent Company is a market leader in providing Recruitment and Interview training for Hiring Managers and Business Leaders. For more information on our training programs
Visit **www.thetalent.co/HiringManagerTraining**

The Candidate Fit Interview Template

No marketer would consider running a marketing campaign without first creating one or more customer avatars that describe in detail who the ideal customer is for the product or service being advertised. In the same way, a recruiter shouldn't start a search without first creating a candidate fit interview template. The candidate fit interview template helps interviewers to spot good candidates and potential top performers. It can be used in advance, while sourcing potential candidates in the market and deciding who to reach out to proactively; in screening candidate profiles and choosing who should advance to the next stage; and during the interview to guide the questions an interviewer should be asking.

Download This Free Guide
For a list of questions to help you determine your organization's own candidate fit profile and sample candidate interview questions
Visit **www.thetalent.co/HiringRight**

You create the template from the output of the exercises in the checklist you just downloaded (you did download it, didn't you? If you didn't, go back and get it now!). With so many variables to consider, however, it is not something a recruiter can do on their own. The exercise has to start at the corporate level, with the Talent Acquisition leader or someone senior in HR—in a smaller organization, where there may not even be an HR function, it's the business owner or founders who need to be involved— and then iterate down through the organizational levels so that the interviewer will be able to assess both team fit and manager fit.

But what about organizational fit?

As we saw in Part One, while the hiring manager is responsible for en- suring a candidate is a good fit for the role, it is the recruiter's responsibility to ensure that they are a good fit for the company. In an ideal world, that would happen before a candidate even gets in front of a hiring manager.

When Recruiters Can't Assess Fit

Some recruiters and hiring managers just aren't good at assessing organ- izational fit, but they may excel in other aspects of recruiting. As you trans- form the Recruitment and Talent Acquisition function, think about allowing people to specialize not only in terms of *who* they recruit, as we discussed in Chapter 9, but also in terms of where in the recruitment pro- cess they get involved.

At the same time, if you have business leaders who are really good at assessing fit, make sure they get involved in every hiring process to provide extra insight and to mentor other recruiters and hiring managers.

Reflective Questions

Are your recruiters able to assess whether a great candidate is the right candidate for your organization?

Do your assessment processes give enough insight into candidates to make an effective hiring decision? Do your recruiters and hiring managers use data and insights from your assessment tools to probe further during interviews with candidates?

How effective are your hiring managers in interviewing and assessing talent? Are your hiring managers able to spot candidates misrepresenting or exaggerating their accomplishments during an interview?

Are your recruiters and hiring managers trained on effective Behavioral Interviewing techniques? Do your interviewers dig deep enough with candidates to uncover the insights needed to make an effective hiring decision?

CHAPTER 12

Offer and Close

Even the best candidate can slip through your fingers at the last moment. Maybe they've been talking to other organizations, or perhaps their existing employer made a counteroffer. It's not enough for a candidate to accept your offer: you need to make sure they turn up on day one, excited and engaged.

By now, you have whittled down your initial list of potential candidates to the specific person you want to hire because you think they are the best fit for the role, the team, and the organization. Now, you have to make an offer and get them to accept it.

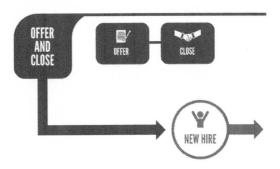

The offer stage is critical in hiring, and yet most companies don't give it anything like the attention, time, and resources it deserves. It doesn't matter how good your sourcing is, how well-trained your interviewers are, how tailored and accurate your assessment processes are, or how competitive your offers of employment are if they don't lead to the best candidate for the role walking in on the first day of their new job with you. So, recruiters need to pay as much attention to closing the candidate as salespeople do to closing the deal. "ABC" ("Always Be Closing") is as important in hiring as it is in sales, and "selling" the organization and the role authentically should be baked into every step of the recruitment process.

Why Candidates Walk Away

It can be a shock for a recruiter when the new hire who accepted their offer either calls a few days before their start date to say they've had a change of heart or, worse, just doesn't show up.

You need to understand that the best candidates are probably fielding multiple offers. And if they truly are top talent, then the chances are that their current employer is also going to try to keep them (indeed, if their employer doesn't counteroffer, you have to ask yourself whether there's something wrong with them). That means that in any offer process, you need to anticipate a counteroffer and ensure you'll be able to compete.

When I was at American Express, I got a great offer from another Fortune 100 company and I was ready to hand in my notice. Then I got a call from our global head of HR to say he was flying up to meet me. Soon, I had a significant counteroffer in front of me—not just more money, but also increased responsibility and authority—and I was getting calls from both the new company and the external head-hunter who were both pressuring me to make a decision.

In the middle of all of this, I attended an off-site meeting in Mexico. When I checked in at the hotel there was a package waiting for me from the head-hunter with articles about why you should never accept a counter offer. I knew he was only thinking about his success fee, not my best interests, and it just felt sleazy.

Once the offer is made, you have to resist the temptation to pressure the candidate for a response. You can present your best case, but ultimately the candidate will make a choice and you have to respect it and stay professional—whichever way it goes.

As appealing and affirming as a counteroffer sounds, I know from experience that counteroffers can actually be very stressful for the candidate. Often, the easiest way for a candidate to relieve the stress and pressure of having to choose is to go with "the devil they know" (even though they had, up to that moment, been thinking of leaving) rather than risk the uncertainty that goes with a new job and a new employer. They have stability, they are comfortable in the environment, and they have built a strong network. It's hardly surprising that they second guess themselves.

When to Discuss Salary

It still shocks me how many organizations let candidates get through the hiring process without asking what their salary expectations are. That can create two problems.

First, the further through the process a candidate gets, the clearer it becomes that the company is interested in them. So, when someone finally does ask about salary expectations, the candidate will feel more confident asking for a higher number.

Second, there's a risk that the company's budget and the candidate's expectations may be so badly misaligned that the whole process has been a waste of time. If you've invested time and effort interviewing someone, you don't want to find out after six interviews that they're looking for $100,000 and your budget is $60,000. And if the candidate is perfect in every other respect, the discussion with the hiring manager is going to be a hard one.

Even large well-known companies don't always get to hire their pick of candidates. It can happen for all sorts of reasons, none of them good. One of our clients, a leading engineering company, engaged us when they were struggling to attract good candidates after being mired in scandal and having the company's name dragged through the press. Another two, a top tech company and a retailer with a long history, hired us after declaring bankruptcy.

For all three companies, the challenge wasn't just how to attract new talent to fill open roles: their existing employees were also worried about their jobs and actively looking for new opportunities. In each case, we needed to make radical changes to their messaging, value proposition, and the offer.

If you're in a similar situation, be open and honest with your candidates, and recognize that you may have to change who you're targeting. The best candidates aren't going to leave a stable job to work for you if they think your business is on the ropes.

You also have to get creative about how you close your candidates. We tried different variations of pay, incentives, and signing and retention bonuses for each of these three clients, and one thing came across very clearly: when your company is in trouble, money up front works far better than promises about future benefits.

In the end, all three companies ended up having to offer salaries well above the market average and a substantial signing bonus, and we protected them by putting in claw-back provisions to recover advance payments if the new hire quit early.

Why Organizations Fail in The Close

The biggest challenge recruiters face in the offer and close phase is that managers simply don't invest enough time in getting it right. Many recruiters and hiring managers don't even start selling until the offer stage, and by then it's too late, especially if you're competing against organizations that have been selling throughout and have already got the candidate engaged with their offer.

Candidates need an offer tailored to them, which means you need to get a good enough grasp (during the Woo phase and beyond) of what matters to the candidate that you can put together a package that checks as many boxes as possible for them.

You also need to manage expectations throughout the process. If you've been open with the candidate in earlier phases, they already know broadly what will be in the offer along with the value proposition for joining the team and the organization, and they are hopefully already excited about it. A good recruiter should never be in the position of offering a candidate $75,000 when they're expecting $100,000: while there's usually some room for negotiation in the offer phase, few recruiters and hiring managers have discretion to jump by 33%, and most candidates—particularly the best ones—feel insulted (and put off) by a low-ball offer.

Making the Offer

When I'm giving a keynote or a workshop, I'm often asked who should make the offer to the candidate. It's easy to answer this if you put yourself in the candidate's shoes. Many hiring managers leave it to the recruiter or the broader HR team. But, most candidates would rather hear it from the hiring manager. That's who they will be reporting to and usually also the person best placed to answer any late questions the candidate may have.

When it comes to presenting an offer to a candidate, it also pays to remember, as we saw above, that good candidates are probably either fielding or anticipating multiple offers and a possible counteroffer. If you don't pay attention to the competition, the chances are they will steal the talent away from you. With that in mind, the hiring manager needs to be prepared for the offer conversation, and the best preparation is to build a great relationship with the candidate throughout the recruitment process. Ultimately, there has to be enough trust and honesty between both parties that the hiring manager is comfortable asking the candidate point blank whether there are any other offers they have received or are expecting, and then following the progress of those competing offers.

Building Flexibility

The key to hiring top talent is always is to make better hiring decisions faster. With that in mind, the needs of the hiring manager, who just wants to hire their chosen candidate, and the requirements of the organization need to be balanced in any negotiation. It helps to have a negotiating plan in place. The hiring manager needs to know what wiggle room there is, any restrictions locked into the organization's compensation structures, and the approval process for any revised offer. Putting a plan in place with boundaries also prevents over-enthusiastic hiring managers from inflating the offer unnecessarily.

Of course, compensation isn't always the determining factor, but often it does come down to a simple reckoning: if a candidate is fielding two very similar offers, but one is for $100,000 and the other is for $105,000, then in the absence of a good relationship, money becomes the only thing they can base their decision on. And if an extra $5,000 is going to be the difference between hiring great talent or losing it, it makes sense to see it as an investment rather than a cost, especially in the context of the organization's bottom line.

Another part of the offer that is easy to forget or ignore is a signing bonus. Because it's paid up front, it can often be more exciting than the same amount offered as an increase in salary—as long as the organization protects itself by making the bonus repayable if the new hire leaves within a specified period—but it's not an ongoing financial commitment in the way that salary would be.

By the same token, don't assume that pay will be the only lever your competitors will pull either. More and more candidates are happy to trade salary for increased vacation time, for example. So, if you're offering three weeks, and another company counters with four, the hiring manager needs to know whether they will be authorized to match it.

Whatever plan is put in place, it needs to be backed up with clear communication between the hiring manager, the recruiter, and the candidate. Revised offers can easily get bogged down in bureaucracy, but even a few days' delay is long enough for the candidate to accept a competing offer, so approval processes needs to be set up to review and present revised offers quickly.

Reflective Questions

How are offers presented to candidates during your recruitment and hiring process? Are there opportunities to improve the offer process?

How does your organization manage and close candidates who receive a counteroffer from their current organization after accepting your offer of employment?

When are salary and total compensation expectations discussed with candidates?

What percentage of offers by your organization are declined by candidates? Why are the offers declined?

Does your organization make the candidate the best offer from the outset or do you negotiate with candidates on the offer?

Are your organization's vacation entitlements for new hires competitive in the market? Are your annual bonus and variable pay competitive? Is your employee benefit program competitive?

CHAPTER 13

Onboarding

Many managers confuse onboarding and orientation. Both terms relate to the process of helping a new hire integrate themselves into the organization. However, orientation generally refers only to the first couple of days, when the new employee is learning how to navigate the organization day-to-day.

Too many companies focus on hiring a new employee without giving enough thought to what happens next. They're not building a plan to make the hire successful and integrate them into the organization. Indeed, only 15% of organizations have an onboarding program that lasts longer than two weeks. For a candidate starting a new job with one of those companies, it's great that they have been hired, but they're not being set up for success and they're probably going to struggle.

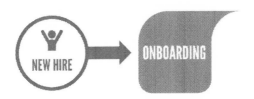

Part of the problem is that managers often confuse onboarding and orientation. Onboarding is the process of bringing in a new hire, helping them understand the company, the team, the environment, and their new role. Orientation is part of that, but onboarding is a much more extensive and in-depth process that the organization and manager need to approach with a much longer-term mindset. The central idea is to engage the employee and continue selling the idea that the organization is the best place to work throughout their first six to twelve months by providing ongoing opportunities to learn, develop their career, and build an internal network. And sometimes even the smallest things can derail that process.

We were hired by a pharmaceutical company to assess their onboarding processes. Most of the company's staff work remotely, so they were flying people in for quarterly company meetings and training, and they had made a significant investment in online learning and coaching platforms to support the onboarding process. However, we held focus groups with new hires and quickly discovered a major complaint: it was taking anything from six to eight weeks for new employees to get their company laptop, so they had no way to access the training and information that had been provided for them.

That situation is hardly unique. I've come across many companies where the biggest dissatisfier to new hires is how long it takes to get set up with their company laptop, but it's a much bigger problem when you've put technology at the heart of your onboarding process!

What Does Good Onboarding Look Like?

Ideally, the onboarding process should start as soon as the candidate accepts the offer. That way, you keep them engaged and excited and they are less likely to consider a counteroffer from their employer or competing offers from other companies.

Good onboarding is not just a matter of putting new hires through a week-long induction program. In leading organizations, onboarding can last anything from six months to a year. During that time, the new employee is being exposed to different aspects of the company and the job gradually, rather than being thrown in at the deep end at the end of their first week.

You have to take a longer-term perspective, agreeing a plan with the individual and recognizing that everyone learns and acclimatizes differently and in their own time. It also helps if you pair the new hire with a mentor or buddy, create networking opportunities for them, and help them navigate their way through the organization.

When I joined on of my past employers, I didn't have the best onboarding experience. On my first day, I was shown to my office and left to get on with things. Finally, in the middle of my second week, I realized that if I was going to be successful, it was down to me. I would have to build my network and figure things out for myself. More importantly, if I didn't take control, I was going to get frustrated.

That's the problem when companies don't onboard new hires properly: they're setting that person up to fail. Ultimately, you can hire the best candidate possible, but if they don't come into the company in the right way, they'll get frustrated, second-guess their decision, and either quit or wait for a switched-on recruiter to reach out to them with a better opportunity.

During the onboarding period, there should be regular check-ins with organizational leaders: does the new staffer have any questions? Are they settling in? Do they understand the organization's business model and how their position fits into it?

One critical way to maximize the effectiveness of onboarding is to personalize it to the new hire. In Chapter 4 we saw that organizations rarely look back at the results of assessments once a candidate has been hired. That's a huge missed opportunity to use those insights to guide and shape the new hire's onboarding and development.

Want to improve your onboarding?

For a checklist of leading practices to ensure your organization's onboarding program will contribute to your new hires' success,

visit www.thetalent.co/HiringRight

Who Is Responsible for Onboarding?

Onboarding is an organizational responsibility, and it starts with the business unit. HR's role is purely as coach, advisor, and facilitator of the process: it is the hiring manager who should create the plan for onboarding the new hire and who should be setting and managing expectations.

It has to be an organizational responsibility because so many support functions have a role in onboarding. For example, IT will need to set up corporate accounts and prepare laptops and other equipment, Payroll will need to set the new hire up in the payroll system so that they'll be paid on time, and Security will need to organize photos and issue access passes.

What does good onboarding look like?

We have created a sample New Hire "First 90 Days" Onboarding Coaching Plan that you can download.

Just visit www.thetalent.co/HiringRight

Reflective Questions

Does your organization have a plan for onboarding new hires?

Is onboarding an HR or organizational responsibility in your organization?

When does onboarding for new hires start in your organization?

Do you solicit feedback from new hires on a regular basis on their onboarding experience with your organization?

What challenges do new hires face while starting with your organization?

How often do leaders check-in with new hires within your organization? How are leaders held accountable for successfully onboarding their new hires?

CHAPTER 14

Engage

You need to keep candidates interested and engaged throughout the hiring process. If you don't, they'll eventually start to question whether this is the right opportunity for them and whether they should even keep talking to you. When—or if—you get to the offer stage, an engaged candidate will also be a lot easier to close than someone who is not engaged.

Engaging the candidate doesn't stop after they've told you they are interested. It is ongoing, throughout the recruitment process. And it's a two-way process. Engagement is not just about deciding what you will say to get a candidate interested; it's about keeping a conversation going in which you probe what it is about the opportunity that excites them, what could excite them more, what else they are looking for, what they already know about the organization and the industry, and so on. All of that information, of course, can be used to build up a profile of the candidate over time in your CRM. The CRM is also your friend when it comes to managing candidates and keeping the process on track.

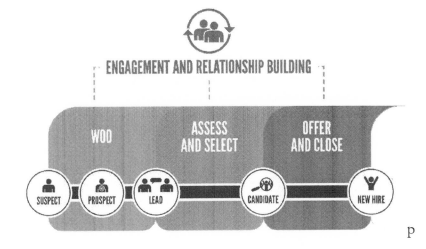

Details Count

As the candidate progresses through the search process, all stakeholders in the process—sourcers, recruiters, interviewers, and the rest—need to be aligned as regards the value proposition, the opportunity description, and the expectations and they need to work together to ensure that the candidate experience is positive and consistent from start to finish, otherwise the candidate will become disengaged.

Engagement builds up (or diminishes) with every touchpoint. When it comes to the candidate experience, other recruiters have set a very low bar, so it's surprisingly easy to exceed candidates' expectation. We've already seen examples of the kind of mistake organizations make: an overenthusiastic recruiter leaving half a dozen voicemails for a candidate they are struggling to reach, or impersonal cookie-cutter emails and long, rambling emails without a clear call to action.

As I said earlier in the book, it's important to be transparent with candidates. Be open about how many other candidates are being considered (and don't be afraid to ask what other opportunities the candidate is considering—it's good to know what you're up against).

One aspect of the candidate experience that many recruiters overlook is how they handle candidates who aren't interested. It pays to remember that you may want to come back to that candidate for a future opportunity, so you should try to leave them with a positive impression of you and the organization. After all, if someone is lucky to get a job with you, you have a recruitment problem: you should be looking for the candidates you'd be lucky to recruit!

Similarly, just because someone isn't a fit for the current opportunity, it doesn't mean you won't have something in the future that they would be a good candidate for. So, you need to ensure that the candidates who don't get picked—the silver and bronze medalists—stay positive, especially since they have indicated that they would like to work for you.

Finally, follow through at every stage. If you promise to call with an update, call. If you say you'll send additional information, send it. And give feedback at every stage. It's bad enough when a candidate submits a résumé online and doesn't get a response. But for someone to take the time to speak with you on the phone or attend meetings and then not hear back from you is unforgivable—and yet, it happens.

Ultimately, the guiding principle is simple: the organization should treat high-quality candidates the way it treats its high-value customers. As with so many other areas of recruiting, it helps to put yourself in the candidate's shoes. You need to understand what's most important to them and leverage that knowledge.

Make Them Want to Turn Up

While it is rare for a new hire to not show up on their first day, especially at senior levels, it's not unknown. The key to avoiding an awkward (and futile) wait on day one, or an uncomfortable call a few days before, is to stay in contact even after the offer has been accepted: the hiring manager and recruiter can't just disappear at the end of the Offer phase.

It's shocking that the only contact some new hires have with the company between accepting the offer and their first day is a letter telling them where to go and when to be there. That's not good enough. Depending on notice periods and other factors, it can be anything from three or four weeks to three or four months from when a candidate accepts your offer to when they start. You have to keep them engaged throughout that time, make sure they understand the opportunity and are excited about it, and address any concerns that they may have.

Leading organizations put in place a communication plan to stay in contact with new hires throughout this period, and they make sure the employee knows exactly what to expect on their first day.

Pulling Back Without Disengaging

At some point, most candidates—all but the one you hire (or however many you are taking on, if this is a recruitment round)—will withdraw (or be withdrawn) from the recruitment process. Most organizations handle this poorly (even if they don't have candidates leaping turnstiles to leave the building), and the biggest mistake they make is to stop engaging with those now ex-candidates.

It's tempting to think of these as "failures" in some way—after all, if they were "good" candidates, you would have hired them, wouldn't you? Never mind that you may have spent hours agonizing over which of two excellent candidates to pick, or that they would have been perfect for a different division that doesn't have an opening right now, or that they simply withdrew voluntarily because their current employer made them a counteroffer they couldn't refuse.

Marketers, on the other hand, don't think like that. Even if a prospect doesn't buy now or turns out not to be a qualified lead for a specific product or service, a good marketer will continue to engage them because they may become qualified later or they may be a good prospect for one of the company's other products and services. And they'll do it using automated emails and follow-up sequences that still make the prospect feel valued, not just a number.

In the same way, a candidate may not have the experience the company needs right now for this opportunity, but they might in the future or they may be qualified for a different opportunity, so the recruiter needs to keep lines of communication open.

And if it's a job profile the company recruits regularly, they might have hundreds of qualified candidates on the books already, but those candidates are unlikely to apply for the role again, especially if they had a negative experience the first time around.

Reflective Questions

How do your recruiters and hiring managers engage your candidates throughout your recruitment and hiring process?

How aligned are the stakeholders in your recruitment and hiring process to ensure every touchpoint with candidates is positive and consistent?

How transparent are your recruiters and hiring managers with candidates throughout your recruitment and hiring process?

Do your recruiters regularly stay in touch with potential candidates who may not be interested in an immediate opportunity but remain open to pursuing opportunitiesy with your organization in the future?

What does your organization do with candidates who are "silver" and "bronze" medalists in your recruitment and hiring process?

What does your organization do to keep new hires engaged between accepting your offer and their start date?

PART 3

Execution

In this part of the book, I look at how to execute on the model I described in Part Two. Recruitment is about the model, the practice, and the programs that help you to execute, and which enable more success in your hiring practices. That all starts with a plan: having a strategy and plan from the beginning will help you be more successful. The plan provides an overall mandate for recruitment, setting out what has to be accomplished in the next year, how it will be done—not only by the recruiters but by everyone in the organization—and what investment will be needed.

When it comes to that strategic planning, every organization is unique. In The Talent Company, we could be working on recruitment strategy projects for two similarly-sized clients in the same industry, in the same city, and we would end up with two different recommendations for how recruitment should be structured, organized, and run.

CHAPTER 15

PLANNING
Workforce and Talent Planning

Workforce planning and talent acquisition planning are about making your recruitment proactive. They're about lining up the recruitment resources the organization will need—sourcers, recruiters, even lists of candidates—before they are required. When you have plans in place, recruitment stops being a matter of waiting for a hiring manager to appear with an open position and asking for it to be filled in two weeks.

One of our clients is a regional electricity company situated not far from several major cities. When we started working with them, we carried out a capability audit of their recruiting practices. We very quickly identified a major problem that they hadn't seen coming: their ability to serve customers depended entirely on the line workers who maintain the power lines. It's a highly skilled job and it takes seven years to turn a new apprentice into a fully competent line worker. However, 70% of their line workers were within three years of retirement, which was going to leave them with a critical problem.

The company had never created a workforce plan or tried to forecast their recruitment needs, and the problem caught them by surprise. And it wasn't a situation they could hire their way out of: they couldn't just poach line workers from other cities, because it would be difficult to get people to switch for the same job with the same pay. Instead, they were forced to outsource the work to electricity companies in nearby cities, which ended up being a lot more expensive than if they had been able to use their own employees.

To make sure it didn't happen again, we worked with the leaders and HR to help them understand how the problem had arisen and we introduced workforce planning. Workforce planning is an HR initiative that translates the business objectives of the organization into internal talent resourcing hiring requirements for a period of time.

The principal aim of workforce planning is to identify broad themes that will inform the talent acquisition plan, for example key skills gaps that need to be addressed or areas where demand for candidates is high enough to merit building a proactive pipeline or talent community. It's about understanding your talent landscape and determining whether the organization will grow and develop talent internally or go outside to acquire talent.

As the gig economy and contingent working have grown in importance, they have added a new dimension to workforce and talent planning decisions: whether to address needs by hiring a permanent employee or by bringing in a contractor. Increasingly, that decision is not only about what the organization wants, however. In some fields it's hard to find candidates interested in permanent jobs; they would rather be independent and contract themselves out on a project basis.

Keep It Simple

The numbers and trends in the workforce plan translate into the talent strategy and from there into a talent acquisition plan (for external needs) and a talent development plan (for internal needs).

The key is to keep things simple. When I was at Accenture in the 1990s, every year we would ask the business leaders to submit their headcount plans for the next three years. The process, as corporate processes often do, had become overly detailed and cumbersome, and business units ended up planning their requirements down to individual hires.

As a result, the information took much longer than it should have done to get from the business, and someone in HR still had to go through it and draw out the main themes about where the organization was going to grow and would need support from Talent Acquisition.

Accenture wasn't unique. Even today, twenty years later, there are still organizations where that happens. The bigger problem, however, is that most organizations never get that far, because fewer than one in five have a workforce plan. That in turn means that fewer than one in five organizations have a talent acquisition plan, because you can't create one without the other.

Part of the reason is that many small and medium-sized organizations see workforce planning as something for big corporations, not for them. That's simply not true. In The Talent Company, our headcount is currently (as I write) fifty, but we have workforce and talent planning discussions every quarter. Whenever we start a new initiative, the first question we consider is whether we have the people internally to deliver it or we need to bring in new people.

Communication is Key

Communication is the foundation of planning. The Talent Acquisition function needs to sit down with each business leader and discuss the plan for the next period, even if all they have is headcount projections and a payroll budget. The other input, alongside future projections, is historical data, particularly employee turnover, which will tell the recruiters what they need to do to maintain the baseline staffing.

In many industries, those discussions can be annual, with check-ins in between. In faster-moving industries, however, like high tech, discussions may have to be quarterly simply to keep recruiters apprised of the latest developments and direction as initiatives change. It also means that

HR/Talent leaders need to be tuned into the sales pipeline and funnel—especially in service industries—and anticipate the impact that significant deals will have on talent requirements.

Recruiters and HR should be holding check-in meetings with the business leaders they support on a quarterly basis. That way, leaders can update the recruiter on anticipated future recruiting needs, new business objectives and initiatives with future resourcing implications, and recurring open roles that impact the business's success. It also gives recruiters an opportunity to validate the roles they are currently pipelining.

The Link Between Strategy and Talent Acquisition Is Two-Way

I am always astonished at how few organizations involve the Recruitment function in headcount forecasts. Too often, it's treated as a pure financial planning exercise, and if Recruitment is included at all it is for their input to the plan, but the finalized projections aren't fed back to them to inform recruitment planning.

When we carry out capability assessments for our clients, one of the first pieces of information we request is the financial plan for headcount. As many as 95% of those clients don't have that data when we ask for it and have to get the information from the finance department.

Similarly, quarterly check-in meetings are a rarity in those organizations. HR managers may have been renamed "business partners" but they aren't equal partners. And even in organizations where HR business partners have a good relationship with their business units, the talent implications of discussions aren't relayed to Recruitment. In the same way, when it comes to new business initiatives, HR and recruiters are rarely kept in the loop by business leaders, even though a large acquisition or the creation of a new division is likely to put significant strain on HR and Recruitment.

Many organizations are driven from a finance or sales standpoint, and in some medium-sized organizations, HR may not be represented at all in strategy meetings. The root of the problem is that talent acquisition is often a low priority for the organization—a situation that I've already said needs to be changed—so they aren't invited to participate in high-level strategic discussions.

Of course, recruiters are unlikely to get a seat at the table even in the most forward-thinking C-suite. But HR should be there, and Recruitment should be able to rely on the HR representative to translate what they're hearing into talent impacts. That HR ambassador needs to help organizational leaders understand why it's so important to be proactive in recruitment and why, therefore, they need to know in advance the strategic imperatives and direction of the organization.

It All Starts with a Plan

Even as the role and expectations of Recruitment continue to evolve, the top two challenges remain the same: capacity and effectiveness. Few organizations, however, have a talent acquisition plan in place to ensure either. Talent needs to be an organizational priority, not just a priority for recruiters. And just like any other strategic priority, every organization needs a talent acquisition plan to guide recruiting activity.

The purpose of the talent acquisition plan is to allow recruitment to be more proactive. If the plan calls for 50 new sales people to be recruited in six months' time, you will need to start sourcing and building pipelines now. That requires a change of mindset by many business leaders more used to thinking of recruitment a few weeks ahead. By putting those proactive actions in the context of future recruitment needs, it allows stakeholders and business leaders to start thinking forward rather than reactively.

Once it has been agreed, the talent acquisition plan acts as the mandate for the Recruitment function, setting out objectives for the year ahead, how they will be met, and the investments that will be needed. Without such a plan, Recruitment becomes what we see in all too many organizations: understaffed, under-resourced, and reactive.

Keeping Your Plan Realistic

The talent acquisition plan translates the business plan and the workforce plan into human resource impacts. It needs to be realistic, otherwise the Recruitment function will lose credibility. Ultimately, of course, talent planning is driven by the plans of the broader organization, so it is only as realistic as the business unit plans that feed into it.

Realistic plans are grounded in historical data: what has been done, how many posts have been filled, and what it cost. So, if an organization has historically seen a 20% turnover in staff then, in the absence of evidence to the contrary, next year's plan should assume that pattern will repeat. If it typically takes three months to recruit a JAVA programmer, then plan for that delay in the future unless something has changed in the market.

Realism also depends on understanding the capabilities of the Talent Acquisition function—carrying out an audit of its strengths, weaknesses, and opportunities to improve recruiting—and relating that back to the changes needed to achieve the plan objectives: if the function is weak in certain aspects of talent acquisition, it will be hard to take it from a 1 to a 10 quickly. That may, instead, require the organization to bring in a third-party firm like The Talent Company to audit, assess, and plug those gaps.

Wondering How You're Doing?

The Talent Company's proprietary Recruitment Capability Assessment™ is a step-by-step approach to providing substantial and qualitative enhancements to your recruitment strategy, processes, tools, program and expertise.

For more information visit

www.thetalent.co/CapabilityAssessment

Getting Buy-In

Earlier in the book, I discussed the need to get business buy-in for the importance of professionalizing recruitment. The Talent function also needs to seek business buy-in and accountability for the talent acquisition plan. First, you need backing from the business for the investments they will have to make in executing the plan. Second, you need buy-in for the future-looking aspects of the plan.

Because recruitment costs were paid directly by business units at American Express, business leaders were direct stakeholders in our team and we were accountable for recruiting outcomes in a way that many recruiters are not. It also meant that, when we were planning, I would have to sit with business leaders and ask them what they needed in the twelve months ahead. I'd then develop a plan to deliver that and tell them what resources and budget I would need to achieve what they were asking for, and they had to write a check for it. As a result, the business knew they had to give me realistic numbers and make me part of their executive team.

Making Talent an Organizational Priority

Ultimately, it is hiring managers who make the decisions. Recruiters are there to manage the process and drive and support the hiring managers in their decision. That means talent acquisition is not just an HR function: the business has a crucial role and, ultimately, it is the business that pays for it.

One of the first steps we take with our clients when we work with them on their talent acquisition strategy is to bring together stakeholders from across the business to act as a "board of directors" for Talent Acquisition, with the HR leader as "CEO." That gets stakeholders involved in the process at a high level and providing their input in a structured, formal way.

As "CEO," the HR leader reports back to the "board" regularly—usually monthly or quarterly—on progress against the plan. Making executives a central part of the process makes it easy to get their buy-in. It also makes it easier to get business units involved in initiatives that cut across organizational boundaries—things like sourcing campaigns, employer branding, and campus recruitment. And finally, it provides a feedback mechanism for HR to get high-level support when, for example, they need to get a hiring manager to prioritize making time for interviews.

How the Workforce Plan Feeds Into Talent Acquisition

The workforce plan identifies where the gaps are in the organization. Then the talent acquisition plan sets out how the organization will address those gaps. Not all recruitment markets are created equal, so that may not always be a simple matter of recruiting new staff. Both geography and the skillset being hired can make a big difference to how recruiters approach a hiring brief, and what it's going to take to recruit the right candidate.

For example, the market for JAVA developers is highly competitive, and recruiting suitable candidates can take a long time. So, organizations may have to invest in alternative ways to fill that need. If the business plan calls for a new IT system, the workforce plan might specify a need for 10 JAVA developers. The talent acquisition plan, in turn, will need to evaluate whether to divert JAVA developers already in the organization, retrain employees with other skill sets, hire contractors, or outsource development to a third-party organization.

Stay Flexible

Many organizations try to plan recruitment annually to match corporate planning cycles. That sets up unrealistic expectations. Market conditions and organizational demands are unpredictable and highly volatile, so while the first three months of a twelve-month plan might be realistic, by months nine through twelve the plan is unlikely to be meeting the evolving needs of the organization.

Many organizations ignore talent planning altogether, and the few that do it often end up creating complicated, rigid plans that are soon out of date. As a talent acquisition leader, you have to ensure the plan continues to reflect what the business requires. I've met too many potential clients over the years who are following a talent plan that was written six months earlier or more. They know it's no longer fit for purpose, but they don't want to re-plan: there is no point carrying out recruitment activities that are no longer needed just because the plan said they would take place.

As we saw above, even Accenture—which was recognized as a leader in talent acquisition practices—fell afoul of this. We invested too much time and energy in creating plans that were soon obsolete, and the annual planning cycle made no provision for them to be updated.

Prioritization Is Key

The good news is, talent planning can be a much less daunting and complex exercise than HR leaders assume it is. Plans need to be flexible and focused, but they don't need to be all-encompassing: it is better to address a subset of resource gaps and get those right than to try to deal with everything and risk getting nothing right.

Most recruiting teams don't have the resources to work on every open position in the organization at the same time. Many of the organizations we work with at The Talent Company only have the capacity to put into action a limited number of projects at a time. In that situation, you have to decide where your time is best spent. The easiest way to select where to focus is by prioritizing the areas which will have the highest impact and return in the shortest time.

The problem with that is that every hiring manager believes their position should be the top priority and they all expect their position to jump to the front of the line. Meanwhile, the organization itself probably expects customer-facing and revenue-generating roles to be prioritized. The answer is to look at what will have the most significant impact for the organization. If you address those positions first, you'll come out ahead of the game.

We'll discuss *how* to prioritize recruiting needs in Chapter 16, when we talk about creating talent communities.

The Importance of Tracking

It's important to track the impact and effectiveness of recruitment activities because, ultimately, the money being invested belongs to the business units. The Recruitment function holds those funds in trust and needs to be accountable for how the money is spent.

I learned the importance of tracking at American Express. Every year, I would sit down with each business unit, go through their plan—including how it compared to prior years—and tell them how much they would need to invest in talent acquisition. Sales is an area where top talent can be particularly expensive, and one year the vice president of sales questioned the value he was getting. "OK," he said. "You're telling me that last year we made a hundred hires. But what does that mean for me?"

I showed him that the new hires were averaging 85% above their sales targets, and how much extra revenue that had generated. He immediately became one of our biggest champions, because I had showed him that we were tuned into his success rather than focusing on our own processes and headcount. It worked so well, in fact, that in future years that VP's question became, "Simon, how much money can I give you?"

Return on Investment

It can be hard to prove a financial return on investment (ROI) in recruiting, but it's necessary. The metric I teach our clients to track is quality of hire. Now, it's always easier to show ROI on investments in roles that are directly revenue- or profit-generating, like Sales, but that doesn't mean that it's impossible to show ROI in support functions.

In those roles, I typically recommend tracking performance against objectives. If a new employee has been set objectives for their first quarter, half year, and year, you would hope that those are designed not only for their benefit but also to feed into the success of the business unit. So, you can look at quality of hire for those roles by looking at how they performed against those objectives, and grading them *Met expectations*, *Did not meet expectations*, or *Exceeded expectations*. In Talent Acquisition at American Express, we wanted as many of our new hires as possible to be graded *Exceeded expectations*.

Hiring Manager Satisfaction

Another valuable metric to track is hiring manager satisfaction with recruitment service delivery. You do that by surveying hiring managers at the end of each recruiting cycle and asking them how satisfied they are with the level of support and partnership they received from their recruiter.

With our clients, we use ten questions, again graded *Met expectations*, *Did not meet expectations*, or *Exceeded expectations*.

**Keen to track hiring manager satisfaction
in your own organization?**

To help measure and assess the performance of your Recruitment function, you can download a straightforward and outcome focused example of a Hiring Manager Satisfaction Survey.

Visit **www.thetalent.co/HiringRight**

Candidate Experience

We saw in Part One that candidates will share their impressions of your company and your hiring process with their contacts. That means you need to measure and track the candidate experience, both for the candidates you hire and the ones you don't.

Of course, when a candidate hasn't been hired, they're unlikely to take the time to fill in a lengthy questionnaire. In fact, they may not even want to have anything further to do with the organization. To maximize your chances of getting a response, keep any survey short and focused and use a third-party firm to administer it.

Scalability and Speed to Execute

Recruitment is not, in most organizations, a steady flow of work. So, the Recruitment function has to be able to scale up and down rapidly as projects start or end. The talent acquisition plan can take out some of the uncertainty and allow Recruitment to prepare in advance for busy periods. It will enable you to predict how many permanent resources you'll need to cope with the baseline demand, decide when to bring in independent recruiters or contract a third-party firm like The Talent Company, and avoid nasty surprises like a hiring manager who suddenly says they need to find fifty people. If you can turn that into "we need fifty people in four months," you at least have a chance of hiring additional recruiters, building a pipeline, and sourcing the best candidates.

The talent acquisition plan should also guide investment in assessment tools, process management software, and even facilities such as interview rooms and rooms for assessment centers.

Building A Recruitment Culture

Ultimately, it is not enough to build a strong Talent Acquisition function—you need to create a pervasive recruitment culture throughout the organization. In a recruitment culture, everyone involved in hiring decisions is aware of the expectations around their contribution to talent acquisition, and this is reinforced with performance objectives that form part of their performance and rewards discussion. It starts with annual goals for the executive team, and cascades down to the hiring managers who report to them.

Reflective Questions

How well does your organization anticipate and plan for its future talent needs? How often do you meet business leaders and discuss their talent needs for the upcoming quarter and business year?

Does your organization do headcount forecasting? Are these headcount forecasts communicated to Talent Acquisition?

What roles within your organization do you consider critical to the success of the business? How well does your organization recruit or develop talent to fill openings in your critical roles?

How effective is the relationship between the business, HR, and Talent Acquisition?

Is talent an organizational or an HR priority for your organization? What can you do to ensure recruitment and hiring are organizational priorities for your organization?

How quickly are you made aware of significant changes to the business and the anticipated impact these changes will have to talent?

How do your measure the impact your talent acquisition practices have on the business? How do you communicate the talent acquisition measures of success to the business?

How can the Talent Acquisition function measure quality of hire effectively for your organization?

Do you measure hiring manager satisfaction with your Talent Acquisition function?

How can you measure candidate experience more effectively for your organization?

CHAPTER 16

PIPELINING
Boost Your Sourcing with Referrals and Talent Communities

In Part Two, we saw the importance of Sourcing in creating a proactive pipeline of candidates. However, even organizations without a formal sourcing function can develop pipelines by promoting employee referral programs and creating talent communities.

Recruiting, as you've probably picked up on by this point in the book, isn't just about new hires. A lot of the time, it's about:

- "The ones that got away"—great candidates you didn't hire, either because they didn't fit the specific role they applied for, they took another offer, or they were pipped to the post by another equally strong candidate.
- "Regrettable losses"—top performers who leave for a competitor.
- And of course, not all losses are regrettable—sometimes the organization breathes a collective sigh of relief when "that person" finally goes. That may not sound like a recruitment problem, but it usually is: with an effective recruitment and talent acquisition function, they probably wouldn't have been hired in the first place.

Some years ago, we were hired by a major multinational consumer goods manufacturer that was suffering too many regrettable losses. They wanted to find ways not only to stop the brain-drain, but also to re-engage with people who had already left. Their head of Recruitment knew they needed to do something urgently but didn't know what that would look like. The answer was to build an alumni program that allowed them to stay in touch with top talent that had left the organization.

Benchmarking other organizations with excellent alumni programs—especially the large professional services firm—we created a program that not only brought back one in ten of those alumni (even three, four, or more years after they had left), but also drove referrals of new talent and created business opportunities with some of the organizations that alumni had joined after leaving. The alumni program has become a major talent pipeline for that client.

The Power of Referrals

In the connected world, referrals are a lynchpin of modern recruitment practice, and an effective Employee Referral Program (ERP) can be the most efficient and lucrative talent sourcing pipeline for organizations. Sadly, most ERPs fail. Organizations spend a lot of time and money on launching their programs with great pomp and ceremony only to have the marketing of the program dwindle after the first few weeks and months and the program quickly gets forgotten by employees.

Employee referrals can be a primary channel for bringing new talent into an organization. That can be a double-edged sword—I've observed many times over the years that good performers tend to refer other good performers, while underperformers generally refer other underperformers.

I saw this first-hand at American Express. In the call center, new hires would go through eight weeks of paid training before going on the floor but they were entitled to benefits from day one. Before I came on board, a lot of poor performers would refer other poor performers who would join for the benefits and the fact that they could call in sick whenever they wanted. On the other side, great talent would refer other great talent because they didn't want to hurt their reputation by referring someone poor.

ERPs have been around for many years and some are more successful than others. In some companies, the ERP is little more than a few posters and balloons stuck to bulletin boards—a glorified 'post and pray' exercise. The best ERPs, on the other hand, turn everyone in the organization into talent scouts and talent ambassadors: people who are proud of the organization they work for and recognize great talent. It's a message that resonates in an environment with a healthy level of employee engagement; when people love working for a company, they are usually happy to tell other people what a wonderful place it is to work.

Where ERPs fall down is when employees aren't engaged and the work environment isn't positive. It's hard to get people to refer if they don't enjoy their work, so an ERP is a useful barometer of what the climate is like in the company.

A great program goes beyond an employee referring their friends into organization. Leading organizations are putting real investment into driving more referrals and adopting a more proactive approach. Typically, organizations can expect to fill around 10-20% of available roles by referral. In these best-in-class organizations, however, that can rise to as much as 30-40% of new hires.

When we help our clients to build a stronger referral program, we make sure they put continuous promotions in place for the program. Too many organizations launch with a lot of pomp and circumstance, and a week later everything goes quiet. There has to be continual communication to employees, not only about the terms of the program, but also about roles that are coming up and the tools and resources the organization provides to help employees make a referral.

One of the major ways referral programs have evolved is that they're no longer just about referring friends and close contacts. Employees are now encouraged to look for opportunities to refer in their day-to-day experiences. For example, we all meet people in all sorts of situations who give great service, even if it's at a restaurant or in a store. If you work for an organization that emphasizes great customer service, that's an opportunity to give the person a card and suggest they'd be a great fit.

At American Express, I was working late one night with our call center recruiting team and we ordered pizza. The person who served us was so great that I just asked the question, "Hey, would you ever look at new opportunities?" The recruiters were horrified that I could be so brazen, but if you say it the right way, it's actually a compliment: "Listen I've been very impressed with the way you've dealt with me. If you're ever interested in a new opportunity, I work for a great organization that does X and we're always looking for good people."

Candidates as Referrers

About ten years ago, I started to see organizations driving external referrals through candidates even before they are offered a position. It's an intriguing twist on ERP and taps into the fact that good candidates often know other good candidates.

This sort of program relies on two factors. First, the organization has to be engaging candidates throughout the hiring process—just as an unengaged employee won't refer, so an unengaged candidate is unlikely to refer either. Second, a little "bribery" doesn't hurt—rewarding candidates for referrals just as you would employees. Just make sure you run any referral rewards, employee or candidate, past the finance department, however, so they can review the tax implications.

Referrals Aren't Just for White Collar Jobs

It's tempting to assume that these sorts of indirect referrals are much easier in a service environment: you meet someone at a conference or training event and you start up a conversation with them about what a good fit they'd be for your company. Like most assumptions, however, it's wrong. Many of our industrial clients find that referrals are their primary source of new talent, even for blue-collar trades. Indeed, in many trades people move around much more than in white collar jobs so they often have an extensive network of colleagues. There are also many training programs where they meet peers just like their white-collar counterparts.

The big difference is that in these blue-collar environments, financial rewards are often a much bigger motivator: a $1,000 bounty will make a much bigger impression on a machinist who makes $40,000 a year than on an accountant who makes $150,000. In the latter case, they're more likely to make a referral just because they are engaged with the organization.

Indeed, in the best organizations—the ones with the most engaged employees—rewards have minimal impact on referrals: employees refer because they're proud of the company, and they are happy to go out to the market and look for others to join the organization. In less engaged organizations, however, rewards become more of a driver.

Rewards provide you with opportunities to encourage specific behaviors. For example, you could increase the rewards for referrals into hot jobs or hard-to-recruit skills. The key is to see these rewards not as a cost but as an investment. Employees are your eyes and ears in the market and, after all, if you hired a third-party agency you would have to pay a significant fee.

When we work with a client to set up an ERP, those are the kinds of factor we consider in designing the reward structure. If they're struggling to find a candidate for a high-demand position, we might suggest raising the premium, which is often cheaper than hiring an external recruiter. We'll also discuss whether rewards should only be given for referrals that lead to a hire, or whether it makes sense to rewards the act of making an introduction, even if it goes nowhere.

Referrals Only Work If You Follow Up

Of course, it doesn't matter how engaged your employees are, and how generous the referral bounties are, if the organization doesn't act on the referrals it receives. Too many programs fail because recruiters don't have time to follow up. When you're under pressure, it's human nature to prioritize a candidate you already have over a potential candidate. Look at it from the referrer's point of view, however. They've gone out on a limb, made the initial approach to a friend, and then they ask them a few weeks later if they've heard from the company and they haven't. It's embarrassing for the referrer, and it disengages them from referring anyone else.

Smart recruiters make contacting referrals a priority, if only because it ensures those referrals will keep coming.

Be Systematic

Often, recruiters don't follow up because they don't have time—or mental energy—to think about how to approach the referred candidate. When I go into organizations, the process for follow up is often the most obvious gap in their referral program. They haven't set responsibilities for following up, timescales, or even what form the follow up will take.

Part of making that follow up easier, even when the recruiters are busy, is to have a defined process. Without that process, referrals will probably just get added to the ATS and lost among the other million names in the database. A sales team wouldn't create a customer referral process and then leave the follow up to chance, and neither should recruiters.

The tragedy in all of this is that, just as in sales, referrals are often a much better lead than someone who applies cold. Depending on the relationship they have with the person who recommended them, they probably already have some idea of the company culture and its employer brand, and their referrer also believes they'd be a good fit.

Make Referrals Easy

One of the big mistakes organizations make in their employee referral programs is making the process overly bureaucratic. As with so much in recruiting, it pays to put yourself in the other person's shoes and go through the process as an employee would.

I've seen companies that expected an employee to spend half an hour writing what amounts to an essay about why they think the person they're referring is a good fit. Not surprisingly, the level of referrals in those situations is very low.

Making Sure Your ERP Delivers

Everything I advocate in recruitment and talent acquisition is about being more proactive and having the mindset of a hunter. In today's hypercompetitive talent markets, organizations can't afford to sit back and hope that an employee is going to refer a top-class candidate. They have to make it happen.

As recruiters and HR professionals, we are tasked with finding great talent, and we must do everything in our power to discover great talent. If we know that top talent refers other top talent, for example, we should be sitting down with the top talent within our current organization and talking to them about their networks and who might be a good fit.

That means creating a talent acquisition culture throughout the organization. Each individual recruiter's role in this is central: they drive the culture by communicating directly with their own network inside the organization and making sure people have the tools and resources they need to make a referral—potentially even coaching employees on how to have "the conversation" with someone they want to refer.

Reinforcing the Role of the Employee

If your ERP isn't delivering the results you hoped for, the fix starts with reinforcing the role of employees in building and finding talent. Employees need to understand that they are the front line of talent scouting and they can help the organization to identify great talent. They need to understand that recruitment can't do it alone, that it isn't just recruitment's job to find people—the organization as a whole needs to be more proactive in building talent networks and everyone has a role in finding great people for the organization.

In earlier chapters, we talked about the impact one 'bad apple' can have on the whole team. That's why most employees want to surround themselves with good talent. Accenture had a rigorous and robust recruitment process. Wherever you worked in the firm, everybody you worked with was great talent, and there were very few weak links on any team. That created an environment where everyone wanted to refer great talent. I have worked with other organizations where the standard for talent isn't as high as Accenture's. People end working with someone, wondering how that person got the job, and you can see the frustration of other members of the team.

So, to me, getting employees to buy into the talent acquisition culture is primarily a marketing exercise: you just need to present the right value proposition, which invariably is about making the organization better. I love the approach taken by organizations like WestJet. When every employee is a shareholder, it creates a culture of ownership and control, and part of that is around who is allowed into the company.

Education and Training

Recruiters need to ensure employees understand the process, not only from the viewpoint of how to make a referral, but also what will happen after they refer someone. That simple step allows the employee to prime the potential candidate so they know what to expect: who will be contacting them and how, when it's likely to be, and what the conversation will entail.

You need to train employees on how to talk to top talent about opportunities at your organization and what it's like to work there. Over the years, HR departments have worked on perfecting their internal marketing pitch—the employee value proposition—which reminds employees of why the organization is a great place to work. Just as hiring managers need to know the message and use it in interviews, the more you can get employees to hear that message and be able to repeat it, the easier it will be for them to make a referral.

The other side of communication, of course, is making sure that employees know who they should be referring in terms of skillset and profile. The more information you can give them in that regard, the better.

Keep the Marketing Fresh

Another way to refresh a failing program is to keep the marketing materials new. Most programs stumble to a halt once the excitement of the initial launch (and the rewards) is over. Programs that work have a marketing calendar that spans the whole year, with something happening every week or month: perhaps new content, a fresh message, a new reward, a new profile of who the organization is looking for. It creates opportunities to communicate and therefore to bring the ERP back into employee's awareness.

There are endless ways to engage employees in the referral program to be talent scouts. The more approaches you can use, the better. For example, we've worked with clients that send out a bulletin every Friday with the latest jobs and a reminder of who they are looking for. The timing is deliberate: employees will be out socializing over the weekend, and when they do they'll be thinking about referrals.

Other organizations use open houses or bring in guest speakers for evening events. Employees are encouraged to bring guests, which is much less threatening for either of them—the referrer and the guest—than inviting them to come for an interview.

Building a Talent Community

Building a talent community is a proactive way to address the critical areas in your organization and the areas where you struggle to find talent. It's a way to get in front of the talent you'll eventually need to find, engage them, and get them excited about your organization. It also gives them insight into your organization.

A talent community is like having your own personal fishing pond. It's a pool of talent that is ready when you need it. Typically, each time a recruiter works on a new post, they start looking for candidates from scratch. Building talent communities lines up the talent you'll need before you need it. Then, when you have an open position, you have already sourced suitable candidates.

Levels of Engagement

In most cases, a talent community isn't a formal group that meets regularly or networks together. They are just a way for recruiters to think about categories of candidates they've identified. People in these talent communities don't necessarily realize that they are in it, although they may have an idea of what's going on—especially since most of the contact they have will be through recruiters.

Some organizations have taken their talent communities further, however, and turned them into industry events, speaker series, networking events, and even industry associations, especially in high-tech fields. The most proactive organizations invest heavily in talent and turn their talent communities into programs with a calendar of events, with the overall aim of drawing as many people as possible to those events. Again, some attendees may realize that they're at a glorified recruitment fair, but many will see it more as an industry or social event.

At American Express, we had separate talent communities for marketing professionals and for sales. We would invite well-known speakers and host 150 people at a time in our lounge after work, and it was easy to get candidates we already had in our database to refer other suitable candidates because they were just inviting them to a talk.

It's something I still do today. At The Talent Company we are always building our pipeline of HR people. While I was writing this book, for example, we organized a speaker series to discuss proposed changes to the minimum wage. We brought in lawyers to talk about the impact the proposals would have on employers, and we were able to attract 120 HR professionals.

Alumni Programs

"Boomerang talent"—employees who leave and then return after a period of time—is a growing sourcing platform for many organizations. Just because someone has exited the organization, it doesn't mean you shouldn't stay in touch. That way, if in the future—whether that's six weeks from now or a year—the employee realizes that their new employer or role isn't what they expected, you can welcome them back with open arms.

The best alumni programs are often a specialized form of talent community. That community might not be specific to a skillset, but they are people have worked with the organization in the past and they are a known quantity: the hiring manager knows their skills, their weaknesses, and their performance—good or bad—far better than they could know an external candidate.

Building A Community

There are five simple steps for building a successful talent community

1. Plan
2. Identify
3. Build
4. Nurture
5. Execute

Plan

Ultimately, you're setting up a talent community to address critical recruitment needs within your organization. Identifying those needs starts with the talent acquisition plan discussed in Chapter 15. Within that plan you target two or three critical areas that will need your attention—for example, sales, marketing and IT.

Once you've decided where to focus, the next step is to think about how you'll build talent pipelines or communities in each of those areas, generate and manage initial lists of candidates, and communicate with and engage those lists. As always, the challenge for most organizations is recruiter capacity. It's hard to build proactive pipelines or talent communities when you are struggling even to be reactive. However, the ROI on being proactive is substantial, as are the advantages of having engaged talent available as and when you need it.

Factors to Consider in Selecting Roles to Pipeline Proactively

Of course, as I pointed out in Chapter 15, if you ask any hiring leader they will say that all their open positions are critical. That forces you to walk a political tight rope to prioritize degrees of criticality. So, you need to work with business leaders to determine which positions they consider critical.

Revenue-Generating and Client-Focused Roles vs. Support Roles

Recruitment priorities need to be informed by what is happening across the organization. Many organizations, as I said earlier, automatically prioritize client-facing roles and roles with direct revenue impact, without regard to the needs of the business. On the other hand, I've spoken to clients who say "We have a challenge with procurement" but their recruiters are focused on growing the sales teams. My answer is simple: "Have you considered hiring procurement people ahead of sales people?"

Recurring and Hard-to-fill roles

If the recruitment function is repeatedly recruiting for specific types of role—often these are ones that are mission-critical for the business—then it makes sense to create a talent community for those roles.

The same goes for roles that are hard to fill. If you know it's going to be hard to find suitable candidates when you need them, it makes sense to create a list of people with these skillsets and engage them in advance. You may make less frequent use of those talent communities compared to the ones for recurring roles, but when the need arises, you'll have immediate access to a stream of qualified candidates.

Functional Experience of the Sourcer/Recruiter

The sourcer or recruiter tasked with building a talent community needs to know the population they're engaging. For example, it's not easy to create a pipeline of sales professionals if none of your recruiters know anything about how to deal with salespeople—you'd need to bring in a recruiter with experience in speaking to, engaging, and hiring sales professionals.

Historic Trends

Recruiters can look back and see what requisitions typically make up the bulk of their work, what requisitions recur predictably, and what skills and experiences are most often in demand by the organization.

External market factors

Recruiters need a baseline understanding of the current candidate market conditions—what roles are hard to fill, what skills are in high demand, etc.—based on their own experience as well as market intelligence.

Headcount projections

Finance are often the first function to be made aware of planned headcount growth directly impacting the budget of lines of business. So, further data will come from financial projections and budgeted headcounts in the annual business plan.

New business initiatives

Business plans often identify proposed new business projects and initiatives, and their anticipated impacts on recruitment.

Identify

Once you've decided which roles to pipeline, the next task is to identify the external talent you want to bring into the talent community or pipeline. A talent community shares certain characteristics, such as a specific skillset, or experience in a functional area or industry—for example, a "financial services" community.

It leverages the research you're already doing for sourcing. As you reach out to the individuals you've identified, some of them will inevitably say they're not interested in the opportunity—whether because the role is not right for them, or the timing, or some other factor. These are people you should also add to your talent community.

In the same way, a talent community allows the organization to take advantage of referrals and cold applications that didn't fit any positions at the time, and great candidates who weren't hired because either they accepted an alternative offer or—although they were perfect for the role and the organization—someone else was chosen at the time.

More importantly, it keeps those contacts warm and engaged. In the normal course of events, candidates only hear from recruiters when there's a new opportunity. In between, there's little or no contact and engagement. Establishing a talent community lets you interact with these individuals and add value to them.

That last point is important: you have to give as much as you are taking. If you're always taking, no one will be interested in your community. You have to add value and give back to the community to keep it going.

Build

Once you have identified the individuals you think are the "best of the best" for the skillset you are looking for, the next step is to build your community by approaching the talent you identified and getting them interested and engaged in your community.

Just like approaching a candidate from sourcing, you have to plan the best way to approach them and the pitch. You become a salesperson, selling the organization and future opportunities to the talent.

The key is to keep communication with these candidates positive and make it a "win-win" for both the candidate and the organization. You need to be honest and set expectations: explain that the individual has been identified as top talent in their industry, but that this is about recruiting proactively for future opportunities, not a current position. Finally, the conversation is also an opportunity to network further and ask for referrals for open positions in other areas.

Nurture

When it comes to engagement and nurturing, technology is the key enabler, and in most jurisdictions the recruiter will need to ask permission to keep in touch as part of the initial contact. Once you have that permission, however, the organization should be sending regular newsletters to each talent community, with relevant industry news and notifications of upcoming events.

In The Talent Company, for example, we have built talent communities for HR, compensation, and payroll. They are separate communities, and each gets its own monthly newsletter with sector-specific news and articles, and invitations to any events we are running for that community. Newsletters like these provide value which nurtures the relationship, unlike sporadic emails or calls from a recruiter to ask if the person is looking for a job.

Over-communication can kill engagement as much as under-communication, and the right technology will allow you to record each individual's preferences about how often they want to be contacted, how, and what with. In the first contact, you can ask whether the candidate wants to be kept informed about each aspect of the community—speaker series, networking events, conferences, etc.—or they only want to be informed of suitable opportunities.

Execute

It's one thing to build talent communities, but ultimately their true value is as a recruitment initiative. I've seen too many organizations that have put wonderful programs in place, but when they have open positions the recruiters forget to leverage the pipeline they've built. That's where the initiative falls down.

Part of the problem is that if a talent community starts to take off, and there are live events that are getting industry attention and a newsletter that people in the industry find valuable, other parts of the organization—marketing, public affairs, event management, and others—want to get involved. As these other functions start to get involved and take over, it becomes easier for the recruiters to forget that the initiative was originally for them.

Building a Business Case

Measuring the ROI for a talent community or referral program faces the same hurdles as measuring the ROI for talent acquisition in general. Ultimately, the reasons for creating these initiatives are (1) to generate a pool of great talent, and (2) to lessen the time to fill positions.

Tracking the success of (1) comes down to showing the number of hires that come from community members and referrals compared to traditional sourcing. If taking time up front indeed allows recruiters to find better candidates than when they have to scrabble around reacting to briefs as they come in, then it stands to reason that referrals and members of talent communities will be hired more often than other candidates.

Tracking the success of (2) is more straightforward: you just need to measure how much faster you are able to fill pipelined positions compared both to how long it took before the programs were in place and to how long it takes to fill other roles that are not being pipelined proactively.

So, the business case for proactive recruitment starts with showing the negative impact of being reactive: collecting data on how long it takes to fill posts, the cost to the organization of having positions unfilled for that length of time, and the level of frustration felt by hiring managers and team members when positions stay open for that long. The aim is to show that, if recruitment can switch to being proactive, the business will be better and employee engagement will increase.

Is your talent pipelining fit for purpose?

For a checklist of leading practices in successfully developing a proactive candidate pipeline

Visit www.thetalent.co/HiringRight

Reflective Questions

How effective is your employee referral program in recruiting and hiring for your organization?

Are your employees motivated to provide referrals by the rewards your program offers?

How can you improve your employee referral program to drive more quality referrals?

Are your employees on the hunt for talent to refer to open positions?

Do you solicit referrals for your open positions from your new hires?

Do your recruiters ask candidates for referrals?

When a candidate is referred by an employee, do recruitment or HR speak to them in a timely and effective manner? Do they do it consistently?

How do you make it easy for your employees to refer great talent?

Would your organization benefit from an alumni program focused on regrettable talent loses?

What critical roles within your organization would you want to build proactive talent pipelines for?

CHAPTER 17

PEOPLE
Hiring Manager Authenticity and Engagement

Candidates have more choice than ever and want to join an organization that gives them what they're looking for. They want a realistic picture of what it's like to work there, not a sales pitch. They need to know the good along with the bad. As a result, true authenticity on the part of everyone involved in recruitment has great power to either excite candidates or scare them off.

I love to sit in the lobby of a company watching employees come and go. It gives you a great perspective on what it's like to work there—if people look like they wish they could be anywhere but there, it's a good sign that it's not a great place to work.

Authenticity is about understanding—and not being afraid or ashamed of—what the organization really is and communicating that to candidates. Technology and social media have made it harder, if not impossible, for organizations to hide their true nature. Social media exposes what it's genuinely like to be a customer of a brand, and sites like Glassdoor reveal the realities of working there on a daily basis and how employees feel.

Being authentic in recruitment is important because it allows a candidate to decide whether or not they want to work for the organization. People will figure out for themselves what kind of organization is hiring them either during recruitment or in the first few weeks after starting, and it's better for someone not to start than to have them realize a month or two down the line that they've made a mistake and they want to leave.

The Interaction of Employer Brands and Customer-Facing Brands

Authenticity in recruitment comes down to both branding and messaging throughout the recruitment process. It is about being open and transparent about what the organization is and what it's like working there. As we saw in Chapter 5, an authentic employer brand taps into the organization's unique personality.

In The Talent Company, when we are working with someone who is going through career transition or looking for a new opportunity we'll ask them which brands they feel a particular affinity for or are most engaged with as a consumer. It's a valuable exercise that gives us a good starting point for targeting potential employers.

Many of the answers, as you'd expect, are well-known companies with strong brands. It doesn't follow, however, that because a company has a strong customer-facing brand they will have a similarly strong employer brand (although in general, it's easier for a company to provide consistently excellent customer service if it has happy employees). In many cases, however, employer brands are nothing like the perception customers have of the company. We can all think of a few organizations that have a great brand externally, but a weak internal brand that doesn't live up to the consumer brand. That can be a shock for a candidate who joins what they thought would be a great employer based on its advertising.

Recognizing the Brand Gap

The gap between a consumer brand and an employer brand isn't necessarily about lack of transparency. Sometimes it's just about the kind of candidate the organization is best suited to.

As I've said, I worked at Accenture early in my career. It's an environment that exposes you to unparalleled opportunities for personal and professional development. Eventually, though, everyone arrives at a stage in life where life circumstances change, and the 18-hour workdays and 80-hour weeks are no longer feasible. The consumer brands of organizations like Accenture don't reflect that kind of thing, so a new hire who isn't familiar with the industry will get a shock unless it forms part of their employer brand.

Smart organizations call that kind of thing out and say, "Hey, we're a great place to work, but also a tough place to work. The bar is high here and the people who'll do well are the ones who want to travel to projects on a weekly basis." What most organizations do, however (and Accenture was just as guilty of this as others back in the 90's) is to emphasize the sexy aspects of the work—jetting around the world to exciting new cities, working on leading edge projects for blue-chip clients—all of which echo the public perception of the industry. They gloss over the realities of life as a management consultant: flying out on a Sunday night, sharing an apartment with another consultant, working all week with no opportunity to explore, and flying back on a Friday night. They also neglect to mention that projects are more likely to be in Fargo or Winnipeg than in New York or Paris.

It's A Matter of Trust

When I deliver keynotes and workshops, I share this research from CareerArc's 2017 Employer Branding Study on who jobseekers trust.

What/Who do jobseekers trust most?

1. *Current Employees*
2. *Reviews by Job Seekers*
3. *Former Employees*

4. *Company Website*

5. *Recruiter*

6. *News Coverage*

7. *CEO's and Executives*

It's a sad comment on the state of recruitment that recruiters and organizational leaders are among the least trusted sources of information for jobseekers. However, the table also offers some opportunities to proactive organizations. It shows that candidates don't want to spend all their time talking to recruiters and executives—they want opportunities to interact with the people who work there, and they want to understand what it is really like and get into the weeds. They just don't think they'll get that from recruiters and executives.

So, the more you can bring current employees into the recruitment process, the better a candidate will feel they understand the company and its employer brand. The key is to impress on those employees that they are not there as peer interviewers—they are there to give candidates real insight into what it's like working there.

What candidates are looking for—from employees and leaders alike—are stories and personal experiences. Getting those people to share them, however, is another matter. Everyone involved in the recruitment process needs to understand that sharing is the key to raising the level of talent the organization can attract and hiring great people. They need to recognize that great candidates need a realistic picture of life within the organization in order to make an informed decision, and that means that they can openly discuss the negatives along with the positives.

Increasing Hiring Manager Engagement

Ultimately, it is hiring managers who make the hiring decision, and they should be involved throughout the recruitment process. They are the cornerstone of the process, not just working with Recruitment, but also making sure candidates think of them as someone they want to work with. Their success in that role depends on them being engaged with the process, engaged with Recruitment, and engaged with the candidates.

An engaged hiring manager is somebody who understands that talent is going to make a difference—positive or negative—to their bottom line. They appreciate the impact talent has on their team and their outcomes, and they approach recruitment with the mindset that the recruiter is the expert.

For the recruiter, engaged hiring managers are easier to work with because they have tend to have more realistic expectations, they are coachable, and when they meet candidates they are authentic and sincere. And candidates leave those meetings thinking *this is somebody I want to work with*.

Unfortunately, in any organization there is only a handful of hiring managers who are fully engaged. The majority aren't, and Recruitment and HR have a central role to play in raising their own level of engagement with hiring managers.

It helps to remember, as I pointed out earlier, that most hiring managers aren't hiring and interviewing all the time, so those activities probably push them out of their comfort zone. A good recruiter can tell when a hiring manager isn't confident in their abilities. That's when they step up to be a coach and advisor guiding them through the process, and to give them the right messaging, the right tools, and the right way to do things.

Of course, there are also hiring managers who hire all the time and see themselves as the expert. They don't think there's anything the recruiter could tell them to do differently, and they wouldn't listen if the recruiter tried.

One of the companies I worked for had two customer service divisions—one to support US customers, and the other to support Canadian customers. Although both were physically situated in Canada, they had very different cultures, driven by the personalities of their respective leaders.

The US leader—let's call him "John"—was focused on talent. When it came to recruitment, he deferred to us as the experts and allowed us to drive the process. The Canada leader—we'll call her "Mary"—on the other hand, had been recruiting for twenty years and believed there was nothing she could learn from us.

The US call center had its share of challenges, but there were far fewer than in the Canada call center and almost everyone in the Canada center would rather have been working in the US center.

Call centers always have lots of HR problems, and employee turnover is high. Ours was 50%, which would be unacceptable in almost any other industry but was about average in ours. When John looked at the US attrition rate, his reaction was "This isn't right. There must be a better way to do things." Mary's view, on the other hand, was that we were no worse than the industry average, so we didn't need to do anything.

I had joined the organization from Accenture, where our mindset wasn't that we were just filling seats; we were seeking qualified people who would be a good fit not only for the role and team, but also for the organization in general. That translated easily into better hires.

When I suggested a similar approach in the new company, John was open to trying it but Mary was happy with the things the way they were.

Ultimately, of course, great talent drives great results, and poor talent drives poor results. Within a year, Mary was replaced—the HR challenges had translated into customer service problems and the division wasn't meeting its performance objectives.

Change Starts at The Top

As my career advanced, I found myself running talent for the Americas and sitting at the executive table with the head of HR and the president of the Americas. The president assured us "Talent acquisition is going to be a priority for all of us," and to prove that it wasn't just a statement, we set aside time in each executive meeting to discuss the status of recruitment, the challenges, and where it was going. Importantly, though, this wasn't time for me to report to the executives: rather, the country presidents each had to report progress to the president.

Leaders need to see the executives above them taking talent seriously and owning it, and nothing focuses a leader's mind more than their boss asking for regular updates on something. As soon as the country leaders saw that talent really was being treated as a top priority, I was suddenly their best friend. The transformation didn't happen overnight, but it did happen

Tracking and Measuring

One of the struggles recruitment departments have faced over the years is that they are often very good at tracking recruitment *activities*, but they don't measure *outcomes*. That blind spot arises because Recruitment falls organizationally within HR, which is primarily a compliance and measurement function. As a result, recruitment dashboards focus heavily on transactional statistics like the number of open positions, how long each position has been open, the cost to fill, etc.

What's missing is any consideration of the quality of hire: how was the hiring manager's experience of service delivery and dealing with the recruiter? How was the candidate's experience of dealing with the organization? Quality of hire is one of the most reliable ways of measuring the success of recruitment, so we need to move from that process-focused mindset to being outcome-focused. We still have to pay attention to the process—otherwise it's impossible to improve it—but, at the end of the day, the outcome has to be more important.

Unfortunately, most organizations don't track hiring outcomes until problems arise. In part, that's because it's becoming harder to get meaningful data to track hiring success. While success in talent acquisition starts at the top—with senior executives holding their subordinates accountable and asking for status updates in every meeting—maintaining the momentum depends on data.

Tracking the process (which is where most HR departments and recruitment functions excel) is all well and good, but it is irrelevant if that process is not delivering the desired results. When executives are held accountable for recruitment outcomes, they don't just want to hear success stories: they want hard data.

Fortunately, recruitment is one area of business that usually has a lot of data to support it. The most basic data is the transactional statistics I mentioned above. Looking beyond that, we need to understand *why* positions are still open: what are the challenges that prevent them being filled effectively and in a timely manner.

Once a position has been filled, we can monitor the candidates who were hired and how they are performing against their objectives—individually and as a cohort. Then, you can set hard targets for each of those metrics and track them like any other KPI, creating a talent dashboard for executive reporting.

Evaluation and Rewards Drive Behaviors

As head of Talent for the Americas, one of the big challenges I had to deal with was how to get business units to share top talent. There were a lot of siloes within our six divisions, and the global CEO had made talent sharing a strategic priority. In the end, the only way I could get the behaviors the CEO was demanding was to sit down with each of our executives and set specific goals with them.

We set up sessions twice a year that we called "talent marketplaces." To reinforce their strategic importance, the global CEO attended every session, and each leader was tasked with bringing two specific pieces of information to the event:

1. Opportunities over the next six months for senior leaders to come into their division and have an impact.
2. A list of their top talent, and who on that list was ready for their next opportunity.

It's usually challenging to get leaders to identify top talent like that, because if they've got a star performer, they don't want to let them go. However, the leaders' bonuses were linked to the outcome of these events and their ability to drive a targeted number of executives into other lines of business. That got their buy-in and made the behaviors trackable. Funnily enough, the leaders consistently met their objectives.

I was fortunate that I had top-level support from our global CEO. Sadly, if you're struggling to get your C-suite to treat recruitment as a strategic priority, you'll also struggle to get traction. You'll need to work with each leader one-by-one, set expectations with them, and sell them on the business case to get them on board. Even if some leaders instinctively see the importance of what you're doing, you'll also have poor leaders to deal with who just don't get it.

Creating Structure

As recruitment starts to show up in the performance evaluation of hiring managers and they want to get more involved, recruiters needs to hold hiring managers accountable for their parts of the process. Even if a hiring manager just asks for a shortlist of the top ten candidates and wants to run the process from there, the recruiter still needs to manage the process to ensure things are being done correctly, candidate feedback and follow-up is happening, and candidates are being continually engaged. Those are things that hiring managers—who are usually focused on the hire and nothing else—will often forget or deprioritize.

One of the most effective tools at our disposal in American Express was drawing up a service level agreement (SLA)—something that is commonplace now but back then was a rarity in recruitment. The SLA is a living agreement that specifies *who* will do *what,* and *when* they will do it. If things are slipping or changes are needed, the hiring manager and the recruiter can sit down and revise the terms, but otherwise it sets out specific expectations on both sides. It's a process that promotes personal responsibility and accountability, and creates consequences for "bad" behavior.

The SLA is also a great tool for promoting communication. Often the recruitment process fails because recruiters don't keep hiring managers updated, and hiring managers make last minute changes without telling the recruiter. The SLA brings everything together and keeps it clear in each person's head. That level of control is crucial for organizations that want to measure the effectiveness of their recruiters. Once someone has been hired into the position, HR can connect with the hiring manager and compare to what extent the recruiter met—or missed—what was agreed in the SLA.

In setting timelines for the process, there's a balance that needs to be struck between speed and quality. Some managers just want to fill their empty post, and they are prepared to sacrifice quality to get a quick hire. At the other extreme, there are hiring managers who will find a good match for their position but want to wait and see if a better candidate shows up. Suddenly, the hiring process drags on, and the post remains unfilled.

In either situation, the recruiter needs to take control. They can no longer be just coach and advisor. They need to push back against the hiring manager and point out the consequences of their actions, whether it's saying, "I can get you candidates early next week, but they won't be the best quality and these are the risks," or "Here's the list of everyone we reached out to, here's what we know about them and about the market, and these were the best five. You've met all five but you're still looking."

Another area where expectations usually need to be set is around providing feedback about candidates. Often, a hiring manager will just say that a candidate wasn't a good fit or wasn't what they were looking for. That's not enough. Recruiters need specific feedback that they can give to candidates who aren't moving further, and it's their responsibility to push back and ask for more detail.

It's All About the "How"

Hiring managers, as I have said, are the lynchpin of recruitment and are often the deciding factor in whether or not a candidate will take a job offer. When a hiring manager is being themselves in the interview, it makes the candidates excited about working with them.

An unengaging leader can do more harm than good. Sometimes that can be because the individual really isn't that engaging, but more often it's because the leader is putting on an act for the interview. In those cases, all that's required may be a word from the recruiter to get the hiring manager to be themselves.

Ultimately, it's not so much about whether you're engaging the candidate as it is about *how* you engage them.

Reflective Questions

When candidates hear your organization's name what do they think of? How does the employer brand of your organization differ from the consumer brand?

Who do candidates trust most within your organization?

How do you evaluate and recognize the performance of your hiring managers?

If a candidate asked a hiring manager, "What do you like most about working here?" what kind of answers would they get?

How can you develop your hiring managers to be more authentic and engaging with candidates?

Conclusion

Ultimately, this book has been about finding the best people and getting them to work with you, and we began with a simple thesis: that great recruiters think and act like good sales and marketing people.

Most organizations (and hiring managers) fall into one of two types. The first type acts as though working for them is a privilege. They have nothing to prove to a prospective employee. Rather, it is up to the candidate to prove themselves to the company. And so, they are happy to post ads and wait for people to come to them. The second type is just grateful that someone wants to work for them.

Neither of those two approaches gives you much choice over who you get to hire. By implementing the strategies in this book, however, you can move into a third group. In this group, you recognize that the best candidates may not be looking for a job at the exact moment you happen to be advertising it. You realize that on paper, even the best candidates may not be a 100% match for your position. And you understand that constant engagement and relationship building is the best way to ensure that, when the time comes, the person you want working for you will take your call.

When that happens, you have taken back control of the hiring process. You have access to the best candidates—wherever they may be and even if they are not actively looking for a new role—and you are maximizing your chances of having them accept an offer from you.

Over the course of my career, I have worked with organizations in every industry, from Big-4 management consultancies to heavy industry, high tech to agriculture. One thing unites all of those organizations: they all

struggle with recruiting, whatever their sector and however many employees they have. When I run workshops and give keynotes, audience members
nod their heads in recognition as I describe this challenge or that problem.
When I ask the audience to list their recruitment blocks, the same things
come up time and again. And the chances are that as you read this book,
you too recognized some or most of what I was describing.

As I said in the introduction, however, that is a good thing. Because
every organization is facing those challenges, it creates an opportunity for
you. If you take the model I set out in Part Two of the book and re-engineer
your recruitment practices around it as I describe in Part Three, you can
overtake your competitors and steal top candidates and top performers
away from them while they—your competitors—are still busy writing their
next post and pray ad.

Register Your Copy of This Book

To help you implement the strategies in this book, I've shared a range of tools, diagnostics, and checklists that you can download as a reader.

Visit **www.thetalent.co/HiringRight** and register this book to download the toolkit:

- **Candidate Fit** – List of questions to determine your organization's candidate fit profile and sample candidate interview questions.
- **Onboarding** – Checklist of leading practices to ensure your onboarding program will contribute to your new hires' success
- **New Hire 90 Day Onboarding Coaching Plan** – Sample onboarding coaching plan
- **Sample Hiring Manager Satisfaction Survey** – Measure and assess the performance of your Recruitment function
- **Talent Pipelining Checklist** – Checklist of leading practices in successfully developing a proactive candidate pipeline

To find out about some of the key support services The Talent Company provides to organizations across North America, visit:

- **Talent Mapping and Talent Pipelining services:**
  www.thetalent.co/TalentPipelining
- **Recruitment and Interview training** for hiring managers and business leaders.
  www.thetalent.co/HiringManagerTraining
- **Recruitment Capability Assessment**™
  www.thetalent.co/CapabilityAssessment

Connect with Simon

If the content of this book resonated with you and you'd like to explore implementing these principles within your own organization, you can connect with Simon and his team:

- By email: simon.parkin@thetalent.co
  (N.B. there's no final "m" on the email address)
- Website: www.thetalent.co
- Connect on LinkedIn: www.linkedin.com/in/simonparkin1

Made in the USA
Middletown, DE
04 December 2018